John J. Nunn

Mrs. Montague Jones' dinner party: or,

Reminiscences of Cheltenham life and manners

John J. Nunn

Mrs. Montague Jones' dinner party: or,
Reminiscences of Cheltenham life and manners

ISBN/EAN: 9783337823597

Printed in Europe, USA, Canada, Australia, Japan

Cover: Foto ©ninafisch / pixelio.de

More available books at **www.hansebooks.com**

MRS. MONTAGUE JONES'

DINNER PARTY:

OR,

REMINISCENCES

OF

CHELTENHAM LIFE AND MANNERS.

BY

J. J. NUNN, B.A.,

AUTHOR OF "SPERO MELIORA," "POETIC WAIFS AND STRAYS,"
ETC. ETC.

LONDON:
JOHN CAMDEN HOTTEN, PICCADILLY.
1872.

[*All Rights are reserved*]

DUBLIN:
PRINTED AT THE UNIVERSITY PRESS,
BY M. H. GILL.

PREFACE.

IN the following pages I have endeavoured to depict the various characters that I have met in fashionable society in Cheltenham in this the latter half of the nineteenth century.

I have striven not to overdraw any of the characters, but leave them, as described in print, very much as I myself have met the individuals. How far I have succeeded I must leave the reader himself to judge.

The critics may raise the objection, that there is not sufficient plot or tale throughout the book; but I presume, that they can hardly blame me for what I have not even attempted to do—namely, to write a complete or sensational novel.

To Mr. Furniss, the artist, I must tender my best acknowledgments, for the able manner in which he has illustrated with his pencil (and thus presented before the eye of the reader) what I have only been able to present mentally.

With a generous "British Public" I now leave this work, having some confidence that it will meet with at least a fair share of their patronage and approbation; and that Mrs. Montague Jones may be found both on the lists of the circulating libraries of the United Kingdom, and on the book-shelves in many private residences.

With the hope that her company may help to wile away and amuse many an otherwise tedious hour,

I beg to subscribe myself,

Faithfully yours,

THE AUTHOR.

CONTENTS.

CHAPTER I.

DESCRIBES MRS. MONTAGUE JONES, AND MR. MONTAGUE JONES ; ALSO MR. WILLIAM SYKES IS INTRODUCED TO THE READER. THE WONDERFUL CURE OF PONTO, MRS. JONES' DOG, IS RELATED. A LAWSUIT CONCERNING A DOG ; MISS DEUXTEMPS IS ALSO DESCRIBED ; AND LASTLY, THE HONOURABLE LIONEL LAZYLEGS, SON OF MY LORD BAREACRES, ... 1

CHAPTER II.

DESCRIBES MISS SMILES, WHO ENTERTAINS A SORT OF TENDER FEELING FOR MR. GUSTAVUS JELLY ; HOW SHE PLAYED ON THE PIANO THE OTHER EVENING, BUT DID NOT JOIN THE DANCERS ; MISS SMILES' ACCURATE KNOWLEDGE OF SCARBOROUGH, FILEY, CASTLE HOWARD, ETC. MR. GUSTAVUS JELLY ; HIS APPEARANCE ; HIS FONDNESS FOR CHELTENHAM ; HIS MIGRATIONS TO HARROWGATE ; THE GREAT NUMBER OF PARTIES HE GOES TO IN THE ONE NIGHT. MISS TIPTOP IS NEXT NOTICED ; HER SKILL AS AN OARSWOMAN ; IS ALSO A GOOD HORSEWOMAN ; SHE BEATS A GENTLEMAN AT BILLIARDS. CAPTAIN HEEHAW, THE "ARBITER ELEGANTIARUM ;" THE MEN TAKE A RISE OUT OF HIM ; HIS STORY ABOUT

	Page.
JONES LLOYD ; HE DOES NOT APPROVE OF EITHER BATH, LEAMINGTON, OR LEICESTER ; CAPTAIN HEEHAW'S IMPOSING APPEARANCE AT THE BALL ; HIS BROTHER M. C. AT BATH, AS DESCRIBED BY MR. CHARLES DICKENS, ...	32

CHAPTER III.

INTRODUCES THE READER TO MY LADY BROADGAUGE ; HER HUSBAND IS DIRECTOR OF A RAILWAY ; HER HANDSOME RESIDENCE AT ALBERT GATE, HYDE PARK ; HER DINNER AND HER GUESTS MENTIONED IN THE MORNING POST ; LADY BROADGAUGE'S ANTAGONIST, MRS. SNARLING ; LADY B.'S COURT DRESS ; MRS. SNARLING'S DITTO ; THE WRITER GIVES A SHORT LECTURE TO THE TWO LADIES. THE REV. MR. DOVECOTE, HIS EASTERN TOUR ; THE ARAB DONKEY BOYS ; THE NEVER-FAIL-TO-BE-FOUND MAN IN THE SHOOTING COAT, WHO TURNS OUT TO BE A " PERFIDIOUS ISLANDER ;" THE NATIVE PHYSICIAN'S CURE ; "ASSOUAN," THE ASCENT OF THE NILE ; ATRA CURA IS IN THE EAST ; THE FLEA ; MR. THACKERAY'S BUG DISAPPOINTER ; A LITTLE GIRL ASKS IF IT BITES ; " MISS BADEN ;" PAPA IS TAKEN IN AT COLOGNE ; MISS PRINCE'S GERMAN IS NOT UNDERSTOOD BY THE GERMANS ; MISS BADEN'S BROTHER TOM READS FOR HIS "LITTLE-OO ;" HE ACTUALLY CUTS UP MAMMA'S BEAUTIFUL PUCE SILK DRESS FOR A RACING JACKET ; HIS PAPA DOES NOT LIKE HIM TO FREQUENT THE GAMING TABLES ; THE " OULD COW'S HORN ;" LADY STIFFNECK ON THE RHINE ; LORD STIFFNECK ABUSES THE LANGUAGE, THE DINNERS, THE ROADS, THE MONEY, AND NEARLY EVERYTHING ELSE IN DEUTSCHLAND ; TOM'S

Contents. ix

ULTRA-FRENCH COSTUME. MR. BRIEF, Q. C., IS NEXT
INTRODUCED; IS A VERY NOTABLE PERSON; THE TRIAL
OF DREDLINCOURT VERSUS DREDLINCOURT; COLONEL
SLIGO'S GREAT DEFAMATION OF CHARACTER CASE; THE
WIT AND HUMOUR OF MR. BRIEF, Q. C.; MR. BRIEF IS
NOT OF A SHY DISPOSITION, NOR DOES HE SPEAK AS IF
THE LAST REMAINING BUTTON ON HIS CLOTHES WAS
FALLING OFF, ... 52

CHAPTER IV.

MISS FANNY SMILES: NOT MUCH WILL BE SAID ABOUT
HER BECAUSE ——. MAJOR GOLUMPUS IS NEXT INTRO-
DUCED; HIS FONDNESS FOR GOOD FARE, HIS GREAT
EXPLOIT IN INDIA, ABOUT WHICH THE MAJOR DRAWS
THE "LONG BOW;" THE MAJOR'S RECIPE FOR A SALAD.
YOUNG DE BOOTS TRYING TO ARGUE WITH THE MAJOR
ABOUT THE QUALITY OF THE WINE. MRS. WHITMORE,
CALLED ALSO MRS. WRITEMORE—MESSRS. SOFTSAWDER
AND DIDDLE ARE HER PUBLISHERS; HER NOVEL CALLED
"THE DUCHESS;" HER POETIC EFFUSIONS, "ODE TO
A ROUGE POT," ETC. THE BOOK IS SOLD AT "THE
LADIES' BABIES' BIB-AND-TUCKER BAZAAR." THE BIR-
MINGHAM CHICKEN GETS A COPY OF THE BOOK OF
POETRY, WHICH HE KEEPS IN HIS BACK PARLOUR.
SIR JONAS BROADGAUGE; IS A DIRECTOR OF THE GREAT
NORTH AND SOUTH JUNCTION RAILWAY; DOES NOT
SPEAK MUCH ABOUT SHARES AT DINNER PARTIES; THE
CHELSEA CHAIN PIER TRIAL; THE BRIDGE IS FLAT, THE
SHARES ARE FLATTER, THE SHAREHOLDERS FLATTEST
OF ALL; SIR JONAS BROADGAUGE'S PORTRAIT, AS SEEN
AT THE ROYAL ACADEMY EXHIBITION, ... 100

x   *Contents.*

CHAPTER V.

Page.

THE SERVANTS IN CHELTENHAM ; THE SERVANTS' CLUB ;
MR. CHARLES HAWKES' SPEECH ; MR. SNAFFLES' INTHO-
DUCTION TO THE SERVANTS' CLUB; A SERVANT GIVES
UP HIS "APPOINTMENT" BECAUSE THE FAMILY GOES
TO HIRLAND, THE CLIMATE OF WHICH COUNTRY IS TOO
MOIST FOR HIS CONSTITUTION, AND HE WOULD, MORE-
OVER, GET OUT OF HIS CIRCLE OF ACQUAINTANCE ; THE
YOUNG SERVANT IN WHITE LIVERY—HIS INEBRIATED
CONDITION ; HIS RETURN TO HIS MASTER'S HOUSE DE-
SCRIBED ; THE AUTHOR'S FAREWELL TO HIS READERS,   148

LIST OF ILLUSTRATIONS.

Drawn by Furniss. Engraved by Hanlon.

	Page.
THE SERVANTS' SWARRY,	*Frontispiece.*
MR. WILLIAM SYKES,	10
MISS DEUXTEMPS,	23
THE HONORABLE LIONEL LAZYLEGS,	26
GUSTAVUS JELLY, ESQ.,	37
LADY BROADGAUGE,	53
THE REV. MR. DOVECOTE, as he appeared at the Pyramids,	62
MISS BADEN,	72
MR. GARRETT, a skilful Attorney,	94
MRS. WHITMORE, an Authoress,	118
THE SERVANTS' CLUB,	148
'ANDSUM JEAMES,	160

Prologue.

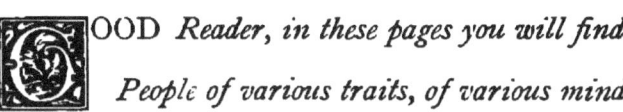

GOOD *Reader, in these pages you will find*
People of various traits, of various mind.
Mrs. J.'s dog will show upon the stage
(For dogs, you know, are still the mark,—the rage;)
In every fashionable house you'll see
A dog recline on mat or on my lady's knee.
BILL SYKES—*with teeth knocked out, of furtive*
    glance,—
Will cure the dog,—a poodle brought from France.
Miss DEUXTEMPS *next will grace the glowing ball,*
And whirl with ease, but not without a fall;
LI. *is the man who shared in the false slip,*
A youth with manhood's early down on lip.

Miss SMILES *is next, with* JELLY *by her side:*
List to his talk, hear now his empty pride.
Miss TIP TOP *see, who shines at hunt or ball,*
Swift in the dance, or neat at four foot wall.
But whose the padded coat? the polished mien?
HEE HAW *is he, the M. C., that's his name.*
Shade of Beau Brummel, *hide your 'minished head,*
Fashion is now by HEE HAW *proudly led.*
My Lady BROADGAUGE *next; and now 'tis plain,*
Her Lord is fond of RAILS,—*she fond of Train,*
A Courtly Train, I mean, not nasty thing
From which SIR J. *his fellows headlong fling.*
But who is this, with cleric dress and mien,
That so much Eastern sea and clime has seen?
From silent college walls, and classic lore
He thence repairs to Egypt's sunny shore:
DOVECOTE *his name; and, seated by his side,*
Miss BADEN *see, with spice of travell'd pride,*
Who lisps of Paris, Rome, the Rigi, Rhine—

Prologue.

And thinks the prospects from the last divine.
BRIEF *is the next,—learned in England's law,*
Pliant of tongue, and sharp at legal flaw,
Whom list'ning Senates welcome with delight,
As fleet the hours fly by through silent night.
Miss SMILES *is next,—both lovely, graceful, fair*
BRIEF *and herself are, sure, a well matched pair*
Beauty and talent see now here combine,
Venus the golden Apollo's bays entwine.
Next is the stern Major named GOLUMPUS,
A man, I ween, who makes a precious rumpus;
If his dinner is not well cooked, quite hot,
He'll doom the cook to most unhappy lot;
Who talks of skirmish, battle, siege, and fight,
And how he stormed the near-untrodden height.
But now, an authoress appears in view.
Her stockings surely are of blueish hue.
A lady's stockings—fie!—what did I say?
I must not speak in such unguarded way.

Know, sir, this lady's shook Parnassus' heights,
With poetic fervour, her ditto flights;
" The Rouge Pot Ode" has brought her praise and
 credit;
Ask each in turn, " have you bought it—read it?"
SIR BROADGAUGE *last, who talks of bulls and bears,*
And of those artful, wily, shares and snares,
Laid to catch those who have abundant cash,
Yet oft they come to most unhappy crash.
Full well I know, for I have dabbled too,
In SHARES AND SNARES, *and do my folly rue.*
And now my song is sung, my rhyming ended,
And if the rhyme is bad, perhaps I'll mend it.
'Till then, this is but all I ask of you:
To give me praise where praise alone is due;
But, if the writing is not good, why, marry,
The pictures must be good, for they're by HARRY.

FURNISS PINXIT.

MRS. MONTAGUE JONES' DINNER PARTY.

CHAPTER I.

DESCRIBES MRS. MONTAGUE JONES, AND MR. MONTAGUE JONES; ALSO MR. WILLIAM SYKES IS INTRODUCED TO THE READER. THE WONDERFUL CURE OF PONTO, MRS. JONES' DOG, IS RELATED A LAWSUIT CONCERNING A DOG; MISS DEUXTEMPS IS ALSO DESCRIBED; AND LASTLY, THE HONOURABLE LIONEL LAZYLEGS, SON OF MY LORD BAREACRES.

READER, allow me to introduce to your notice Mr. and Mrs. Montague Jones, who reside in Cheltenham, at Montpellier House, a spacious residence in the outskirts of Cheltenham. With your permission, I shall first describe

Mrs. Jones, as she is a great deal more than Mr. Jones' better half, he being merely a fraction, while Mrs. J. is the sum total, or nearly so.

Ill-natured people (and there are always some of these everywhere) say that Jones' name is Benjamin Jones, or as the people in the city used to call him, "Big Jones"— *a lucus à non lucendo*—and that, after he married Mrs. Jones, he suddenly came out as Mr. Montague Jones. Certainly there are no Montagues on his side of the house, and there are very grave doubts if there be any on Mrs. Jones' side either. But, however, let this pass.

It is quite a curiosity to see Mr. and Mrs. Jones walking down the promenade in Cheltenham. You would think that they must somehow have changed places—that he would make a better woman than Mrs. Jones, and that she would make a decidedly fine man, of the jolly, well-fed, good-natured sort. Then there was Ponto, their dog, a large white French poodle, whom every boy in Cheltenham knew, and whom they would call after by name.

Mrs. Jones, when she engaged a man-servant, always made it a point to ask if he understood the management of dogs, as he would be expected to wash and dress Ponto, and look after his wardrobe—the said wardrobe consisting of a jacket, which was attached to his person during the winter, something like a racehorse's clothing, minus the clothing for the neck. He had also to be clipped from time to time, but this important operation was entrusted to a French canine artist in London, who had entirely gained the confidence of Mrs. Jones, though there was another artist, who resided about the Pont Neuf, in Paris, who was highly extolled also. Monsieur Friponnier was the artist's name: if any of my readers should require his services, or rather any of my readers' dogs. Poor Ponto's stomach being deranged last season, the Cheltenham doctor, Dr. Softly, M. D., author of many learned works on the stomach and intestinal canal, was consulted. Of course it was quite a favour that Dr. Softly came at all; but Mrs. Jones entreated him to come and see her favourite, and Softly accordingly came; but as Mrs. Jones herself felt indisposed that day, the dog medicine and his mistress' recipe were written on the same elegant gold-edged note paper.

But, alas, Dr. Softly, author of "Diseases of the Intestinal Canal," and other works, was unable to effect a cure. Ponto would growl at the Doctor in a defiant manner, show a row of very white teeth, and contrary to the usages of his country,[1] act in a most discourteous manner towards a stranger: indeed, at times, the Doctor's

---

[1] The reader is requested to remember that Ponto came from La Belle France.

leg appeared in imminent danger of being transfixed by the before-mentioned white teeth.

But the cure that could not be effected by Mr. Softly was effected by Mr. William Sykes—or as he is familiarly called, Bill Sykes—of Blackfriars-road, London. I am not aware that Mr. Sykes has studied in any college. Mr. Sykes' mode of entering a room was peculiar—quite different from Dr. Softly, M. D.'s elegant manner. Mr. Sykes' appearance was not very prepossessing, his hair being cut very short, so that it appeared as if it were clipped as close as it possibly could with a scissors, without injuring the head; at each side, on the cheek, he had a twist of hair, curled round almost into a circle, oiled and greased into uncommon stiffness; his trowsers were very tight, and his feet encased in highlows; several of his front teeth were knocked out; and, to a judge's eye, he looked very much like a member, or rather ex-member of the P. R. It was the Honourable Lionel Lazylegs who introduced Mr. Sykes to the notice of Mrs. Montague Jones.

The Honourable Lionel is, as all the world knows, son of my Lord Bareacres, and became acquainted with Sykes whilst pursuing his studies at Oxford, which, as report speaks, came to an abrupt termination after the first Term only was passed, and a career of much promise (as he himself says) brought to an untimely conclusion. After much persuasion, Mrs. Jones, when in London for the season, was induced to let Mr. Sykes take Ponto away with him; and Mr. Sykes declared on oath (a habit to which he was somewhat addicted), and promised before several witnesses, that he would not starve or ill-treat Ponto. But, sad to relate, though Ponto came back cured of the internal derangement, he now appeared so dreadfully thin that his mistress was inconsolable; and, indeed, on his first showing his new figure to Mrs. Jones, that kind-hearted lady burst into tears.

I have been thus far discursive about

Ponto, because he is so important a personage in Montpellier House that it would be quite incomplete to write about Mr. and Mrs. Jones, and not give some account of the mighty Ponto.

I would, if time permitted, have told also all about the trial that took place about Ponto, on account of the exorbitant demand made by Professor Sykes for the cure of the dog. Messrs. Catchim, Shakehim, and Tearim, the eminent attorneys, employed Mr. Charles Busfuz, a near relation of that eminent luminary of the law, mentioned by Mr. Charles Dickens, who delivered a most powerful speech. I have no doubt it is printed in full in the morning papers, and, perhaps, has found its way into the Law Reports. Ah, here it is, reader—how fortunate, I have just found it.

"*William Sykes* versus *Montague Jones.*"

"This was an action brought by the plaintiff, who described himself as a 'Canine Doctor,' against the defendant, who resides at Cheltenham. Plaintiff had an infirmary for dogs in the neighbourhood of Blackfriars-road, London. He was given the dog to cure of gross obesity and derangement of the stomach. The defendant, when in London, drove to his establishment, and said she had at last resolved to entrust the dog to his care, to have its some-

Mr. William Sykes.

Portrait of Mr. Sykes, as he appeared after the verdict given against him (Sykes *versus* Montague Jones). [p. 10.

what extravagant proportions reduced, et cetera.

"So the plaintiff took charge of the sufferer, removed its obesity and derangement of the stomach, and brought back the animal to the defendant. When he did so, he was asked his charges, and was then only offered (what do you think, reader?)—£15. This offer he spurned, as if an indignity had been offered him: his fee was not £15, but £25. The defendant had the ingratitude to lodge only this paltry £15 in Court.

"Plaintiff was examined by Mr. Wordyman, Q.C.

"Is a professor of the art of curing

dogs ; he was shocked and hurt at the behaviour of the defendant. In place of settling an annuity of £100 a year upon him for his services [laughter], they thought to put him off in this *contemptible* way; it was all very well until the dog was cured. Plaintiff took the brute to sleep in his own room, and used to get up to attend on him at midnight [laughter]; he had been most successful, and brought the dog back again to Mrs. Jones in London. When he gave the dog up, Mrs. Jones asked his charge, when he replied £25. 'O,' she said, 'that is exorbitant,' and she only offered him £15. Plaintiff refused to take it, and she desired him to come again on the following morning; he did go, and met Captain Hee Haw there; and even the £15 the Captain would not give him, although the dog got the best of beefsteaks at 1s. a pound, and most expensive medicines for twenty-one days into the bargain.

"Charles Hawkes, examined, and proved the delivery of the dog to plaintiff. This witness proceeded to state, that his mistress, when she brought it to be cured, kissed it and wished it good bye, as if it was a Christian; and said 'God bless you, Ponto' [roars of laughter, in which the learned Judge appeared to join].

"Mr. Serjeant Busfuz denounced the

bringing of this case into the Superior Courts. It might have been disposed of by the County Chairman for a few shillings; as for the merits of the plaintiff's case there were none. Captain Hee Haw, the respected master of the ceremonies at Cheltenham, would be examined, who would prove that this soi-disant professor had told him that the dog drank two guineas' worth of the best port.

"As to any ridicule being cast upon Mrs. Jones, his client, for her love for her dog, he (Mr. Serjeant Busfuz) could see no cause for laughter. That eminent man, Dugald Stewart, in his work on 'Moral Philosophy,' speaking of the 'Desire of Society,' says, p. 33 :—

"'We feel ourselves in an unnatural state when in a state of solitude, and, by making companions of the lower animals, or by attaching ourselves to inanimate objects, strive to fill up the void of which we are conscious.'

"Mrs. Jones, I am sure, when Mr. Jones has been at his club, has felt this void, this blank, filled up by the caresses of the now famous Ponto. Gentlemen of the jury, was it unreasonable, I ask, that my client should endeavour, when she saw Ponto's once graceful, lithe figure growing coarser and more rotund every day—was it unreasonable, I ask, when she saw that his jackets were no longer large enough to protect his body from the cold of our northerly climate—was it absurd to endeavour to reduce his proportions, and make him once more an object of attraction and admiration to the promenaders in Cheltenham? I fearlessly answer, and I am sure it would be your own answer also —certainly not.

"*A verdict was given for defendant.*"

And now, dear readers, to some of you I must pen a little sermonette. While many of you, like Mrs. Montague Jones, cry over the sickness of your dogs, and pay £15 to get them cured of their grossness, do you attend to the sick of your own species? Do you pay a single £15 per annum?—nay, a single £5 per ditto?—nay, a single £1 per ditto for the relief of your sick neighbours? Whilst some of you attend to your "Tiny's" or your "Ponto's" jackets, do you also try to clothe the naked? Ponto has at least a natural jacket of hair, but remember many BIPEDS there are who have no decent clothing to keep out the winter's cold.

Should not, then, many of us cry "Peccavi," "Peccavi?"

You see I have not penned a long sermon, but it is pithy, I hope.

And now, as I have concluded the discourse with the renowned Ponto, and Mrs. Montague Jones for my text, I beg to be permitted to resume, and will, therefore, hasten to describe those that were asked to the dinner party, and the conversation and manner of the guests.

Before I proceed further, I beg to present my readers with the accompanying diagram, which, I hope, will tend to show clearly the manner in which the guests were disposed at the hospitable board of Mrs. Montague Jones:—

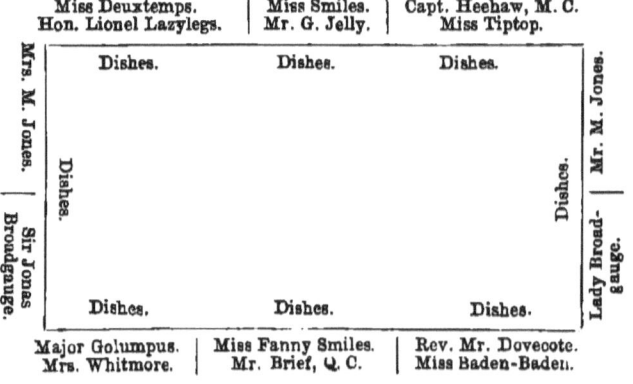

Mr. Montague Jones is, as we before said, in stature very small; he appears to be quite under the orders of Mrs. Jones, who is the devotee of fashion. Mr. Jones is rather, or, indeed, altogether, inclined for quietness, but acquiesces in all Mrs. Jones' wishes for fashionable life with a good-natured acquiescence.

Mr. Jones would rather prefer a country life, with farming,[1] magisterial duties, poor-law boards, &c., but Mrs. Jones says she would die of *ennui* in the country, so Jones has, as many other

---

[1] Unmindful of the lines which run thus:—
"He that would drive fat oxen
Should himself be fat."

men have done before him, given up to his wife. He has, however, his garden, of which he is fond, and an extraordinary fancy for cockatoos, of which he has no less than twenty-five at the least; these are prized for the beauty of their plumage, and are to be seen on a fine day ranged along a wall, sitting on the top of which they enjoy the sunshine, each with a chain to his leg. The light blue plumage, the red and blue, and, above all, a beautiful white bird, with a tinge of salmon colour under the wings, is the admiration of all beholders.

An odd taste, some will say, for a man to have, to keep all these birds;

nevertheless, Mr. Jones would not part with his birds on any account; and, as Mrs. Jones has Ponto as a pet, Mr. Jones contends he has a right to his twenty-five cockatoos.

Mr. Jones keeps a couple of hunters; but his hunting consists principally in riding out to meet the hounds, and riding along roads so as to nick in with the hounds, certainly not in riding across country. He often, with Mrs. Jones, has some lady to escort, and he is very good-natured, as when asked he always takes charge of any lady who wishes an escort, being known to be most steady and considerate.

Sometimes Mrs. Jones drives to the

meet with phaeton and pair of ponies. Often the ladies get up large riding parties to ride to Gloucester or Sudely, or the racecourse, or some such place; and even on hunting days, and a good meet, Jones will be seen as one of the party.

Jones keeps up a running fire of small talk about the London season that is just beginning; about the opera; his club, the dinners there; the park, and who had the best turned-out carriage; about Spurgeon; the debates in the house; about Gladstone, D'Israeli, Lowe, Lord Stanley; the late Abyssinian war; then of Baden-Baden — the roulette tables; the table d'hôte; the couriers,

Miss Deuxtemps. [p. 23.

passports, picture galleries; the best route to the Rhine, Paris, &c.

Miss Deuxtemps.

We will now glance round the table, and you will perceive Miss Deuxtemps and the Honourable Lionel at the left of the hostess. With the reader's permission I will describe them first, after the host and hostess, and thus go round the table from this starting-point.

Place aux dames! Miss Deuxtemps is, as her name intimates, rather a rapid young lady—she delights in fast dances; and the Honourable Lionel is quite up to the mark in rapidity. Indeed, after the champagne has circulated at supper, the Honourable Lionel's gyrations are of the most astounding rapidity; he has been known to quite tire down the whole of the dancers at a ball, and, with Miss Deuxtemps, to be the last to leave off in the waltz; the fiddlers could fiddle no more, but if the fiddlers' arms were tired out, not so the Honourable Lionel's legs; indeed, though he had a habit of lounging about in the streets, he could quite change when under the inspiration of Terpsichore. Miss Deuxtemps dances a great deal with fast cavalry officers, and talks with rapture of the delightful season she spent at Brighton, and the splendid ball given by the 7th Hussars when she was there.

On a late occasion Miss Deuxtemps and her partner were waltzing, when they came in contact with a couple who had just left off, and so great was the force of the collision that they knocked the couple down, and, as the newspapers would say, when speaking of a railway accident, precipitated them a considerable distance along the line.

"Nec dulces amores
Sperne, puer, neque tu choreas."

Miss Deuxtemps and the Honourable Lionel have a kind of standing flirtation always on. Indeed the Honourable Lionel has a very graceful way of paying compliments. Miss D. was just now saying how much she liked early rising in summer.

"Ah," said the Honourable—

"'Clarissa, early on the lawn,
    Steals roses from the blushing dawn.'"

Miss D.—"Now, do be quiet with your nonsense."

THE HONOURABLE LIONEL.

I cannot help saying that I have a considerable partiality (like nearly every one else) for the Honourable Lionel; he has such a fund of good humour, and is so unaffected withal, that a stranger cannot help liking him even on a short acquaintance.

The Honorable Lionel Lazylegs. [p. 26.

I think we have gained a little insight into his Oxford career, to which University he went after leaving Eton.

Lord Bareacres had great hopes of his second son becoming a member of the bar, and he hoped a distinguished member; but the Honourable Lionel was much more addicted to the study of dogs, horses, and rats, and pugilistic encounters, than the study of Virgil, Horace, Demosthenes, or Plato.

Idle though he is, he has considerable abilities. In person he is of good height, fair complexion, hair of a light brown, and he is graceful and gentlemanlike in demeanour.

It is understood that there is a quarrel

between the father and son, but the Honourable has had some cash left him by his mother, and he thinks he will spend this at all events in Cheltenham. Mr. William Sykes is a great admirer of the Honourable, and is supposed to have initiated him into the art of self-defence at Oxford: "For," said Mr. Sykes, "every ge'man ought to know how to defend hisself, caze, ye see, he can't tell when a row may turn up." But the Honourable Lionel has given up the cæstus, as suited only for Freshmen, and devotes his time and talents to the turf. Snaffles, his groom, is a great assistance to the Honourable, being a discarded hanger-on about a racing stable, in which he carried on some very fishy practices, and was generally supposed to have had the principal hand in administering croton oil to a leading favourite for the Derby some years ago. Snaffles, however, has become more circumspect, and alludes to his youthful days as a period of his life when he was young and foolish. Mr. Snaffles is a member of the Servants' Club, and is one of the managing committee of that institution, which is held at a neighbouring green-grocer's in a central position in the town. But we are digressing.—The Honourable Lionel has been somewhat fortunate on the turf, as he has won a good sum on a recently run Derby, and has figured successfully across country on his own horse, called "Binks the Bagman."

Miss "Deuxtemps" does not like the name, and teases the Honourable to change it, but on this point he is inexorable. Mr. Snaffles prides himself very much on the high state of training that Binks had been got into; but I think as much credit is due to the Honourable for the way he rode his horse. But, dear reader, if, as I have already said, the Honourable Lionel is not inclined to study Virgil, Horace, Demosthenes, or Plato, yet, in effect, he follows the advice of the cheerful Flaccus; for does not the said Flaccus write as follows, and does not the Honourable pursue the advice so admirably rendered into English by Professor Conington? Here it is—

> "Oh, ask not what the morn will bring,
>   But count as gain each day that chance
> May give you; sport in life's young spring,
>   Nor scorn sweet love, nor merry dance,
> While years are green, while sullen eld
>   Is distant; now the walk, the game,
> The whisper'd talk at sunset held,
>   Each in his turn prefer their claim.
> Sweet, too, the laugh, whose feign'd alarm
>   The hiding-place of beauty tells;
> The token ravish'd from the arm,
>   Or finger, that but ill rebels."
>
> CONINGTON'S *Horace*.

CHAPTER II.

DESCRIBES MISS SMILES, WHO ENTERTAINS A SORT OF TENDER FEELING FOR MR. GUSTAVUS JELLY; HOW SHE PLAYED ON THE PIANO THE OTHER EVENING, BUT DID NOT JOIN THE DANCERS; MISS SMILES' ACCURATE KNOWLEDGE OF SCARBOROUGH, FILEY, CASTLE HOWARD, ETC. MR. GUSTAVUS JELLY; HIS APPEARANCE; HIS FONDNESS FOR CHELTENHAM; HIS MIGRATIONS TO HARROGATE; THE GREAT NUMBER OF PARTIES HE GOES TO IN THE ONE NIGHT. MISS TIPTOP IS NEXT NOTICED; HER SKILL AS AN OARSWOMAN; IS ALSO A GOOD HORSEWOMAN; SHE BEATS A GENTLEMAN AT BILLIARDS. CAPTAIN HEEHAW, THE "ARBITER ELEGANTIARUM;" THE MEN TAKE A RISE OUT OF HIM; HIS STORY ABOUT JONES LLOYD; HE DOES NOT APPROVE OF EITHER BATH, LEAMINGTON, OR LEICESTER; CAPTAIN HEEHAW'S IMPOSING APPEARANCE AT THE BALL; HIS BROTHER M. C. AT BATH, AS DESCRIBED BY MR. CHARLES DICKENS.

Miss Smiles

TS a young lady of *enbonpoint* appearance. She is, as her title denotes, the elder of the two sisters, and considers, therefore, we presume, she should go off first (I mean in matrimony). *En passant*, dear reader, how is it that in some families, where two young ladies are going out, and the younger of the two is considerably the nicer-looking and more agreeable, that, if any young man approaches, it is, nevertheless, expected that he should devote his attentions (especially if of any serious nature) to the elder only. Her sister, Miss Fanny Smiles, is the taller, slighter, and in every way the nicer-looking, so that, I regret to say, she gets better and more partners than her elder sister. Miss Smiles does not, therefore, look on her sister with entire approbation, but thinks she is forward, and laughs too loud at times. Miss Smiles has been making some preliminary attacks on the heart of Gustavus Jelly; but Gustavus will, in the writer's opinion, and in that of many others, go on probably for the next fifty years as he is doing now, and matrimony is not what comes within the range of his philosophy. Gustavus and Miss Smiles are certainly somewhat suited to each other, as in point of intellectual endowments they are very much on a par, and their talents, when clubbed together, would not be overpowering.

But to make up for some outward failings, Miss Smiles has a very good knowledge of music, and her touch and execution on the piano are beyond mediocrity. Miss Smiles is very good-natured about her playing, as the other day she played for a considerable time (which I myself was witness of) for some dancers—indeed it altogether prevented her dancing; to be sure, the Honourable Lionel, who could not join at all (on account of a fall he got out hunting), was the greater part of the evening sitting at the piano near her; but, surely, that had nothing to say to the matter at all.

Miss Smiles has just been conversing with Mr. Jelly about Scarborough, and talking especially of the castle there, and of the hotels, and which is the best, and of the Crown Hotel and the table d'hôte; and of Flamborough Head, and York Minster, and of Filey and Whitby, and the jet ornaments; and Lord Carlisle's Seat (Castle Howard), and the picture of the Three Marys, and how it is hid in the wall; and the shameful way that the people ride on the strand with the hired horses, to the great risk of life and limb of those that are walking; and how she made a collection of seaweed; and how such thousands come by train to Scarborough from York, Manchester, Leeds, &c., &c., and then find that there is no room in the town, and that they have, as a last resource, to hire a

Gustavus Jelly, Esq.

bathing-box at a fabulous price to sleep in.

All this kind of conversation Gustavus Jelly can quite enter into, as he knows nearly every watering-place in England of any note.

MR. GUSTAVUS JELLY.

Mr. Jelly is in stature of middle height, has fair and quite straight hair, which he divides in the centre; whiskers also fair and well brushed out; his complexion is pink and white, and on which the late hours and heated rooms seem to have had little or no effect. He is particularly neat in his dress and person, and is, I suppose, what some ladies would term a nice young man. At first you would think favourably of him; but, alas! he has that lisping and unmeaning voice that betrays the character of the man. He sings a little, plays a little, flirts, rides, and dances; he considers himself quite an authority about ladies' dresses, has a great deal of small talk, and thinks that a watering-place like Cheltenham is the only fit place for a man to live in.

Not that he is always in Cheltenham; far from it. Mr. Jelly, as I said before, knows nearly every watering-place in England; and so nicely does he adjust the time, that, when the gaiety is over in Cheltenham, he migrates to some other place where the season is coming on. Harrogate sees him often in the autumn, and he is generally on the ball committee at the Green Dragon. Mr. Jelly is more ornamental than useful, and belongs to the non-laborious and non-industrial class, for they " toil not, neither do they spin."

The number of parties that Mr. G. J. attends in one evening is to me quite astounding. I reckoned them the other day, and the number of visits, &c., quite upset me.

First, Mr. G. J. went to pay some morning calls (this was merely a little trifling affair); then came a flower show at 3 o'clock; then a dinner party at

Mrs. Goldplas', at 7 o'clock; then a musical at Mrs. Dolche's, where the great Signor Tenori sung at a fee of twenty-five guineas the night, and four songs only allowed; then a ball at Imperial-square; then another in Lansdowne-place; then another at 37, Promenade, where he what is termed looked in at; then G. J. gravitated to Pittville, where he finished the ball-going part of the evening; and then concluded, with oysters, porter, and devilled bones, at the Imperial Club, a tolerably good day's work, one would say, when kept up every day in the week.

Miss Tiptop.

Miss Tiptop is the only daughter of a Yorkshire baronet, and has derived from her father and brothers a great taste for sporting of all kinds ; her mother is an invalid (or rather considers herself such), and Miss Tiptop has, consequently, been thrown very much amongst the society of her brothers and father.

With all her sporting tastes, Miss Tiptop is quite the lady. On a recent occasion the writer was with a friend visiting her father at Hampton Court, where they had taken a house by the year, when, being on the river, I was quite astonished at Miss Tiptop's skill as an oarswoman. She appeared quite able to steer, row, back water, and perform any of the mysteries of aquatic life.

Nor was this all, for my friend, having rashly accepted a challenge to a game of billiards, Miss Tiptop beat him in the most ignominious manner. In spite of all his excuses about not knowing the table, I suspect he was no match for Miss Tiptop.

But it is in the hunting field that my heroine shines conspicuously; she is a true scion of the Tiptop family; for, as the tenants say, there never was one of them that could not ride well.

Her father has been for a long time a master of fox hounds. She talks of the great Dunchurch run with the Warwickshire, of the Crick run with the Pitchley, and the Bilsdon Coplow run, as if she herself had partaken of the sport.

Miss Tiptop is at present in high glee at the prospect of being one of the riding party in the morning that are to go to the meet of the Cotswold, at the six-milestone on the London road. Miss Tiptop is going to ride on her own mare, Norma, whilst Miss Deuxtemps has arranged with Mr. Reeves for the best lady's mare in his stable.

Captain Heehaw.

Captain Heehaw, M. C., and "Arbiter Elegantiarum"—for he is binomial—is, of course, a well-known character in Cheltenham ; he is devotedly attached to the town, and thinks that the words of a local bard are absolutely true that commence thus—

> "Where is the town in all this land
> Can be compared to Cheltenham ?"

He is a man of tall and commanding appearance, and has a perpetual smile hovering about his smooth and well-shaved countenance ; he can talk of military matters to the men, also about the Cotswold Hunt, the Oxfordshire and

Sir Maurice Berkeley's; and with the ladies he can talk about the last ball and the forthcoming ones; about the dinner parties, and who was there, and all kinds of divers local matters.

The men often take a rise (as they call it) out of Heehaw about other watering-places. The Honourable Lionel, the other day, when in company with Captain Raff, thus began:—

"I declare, Heehaw, I think I shall go to Leamington next winter, to hunt there. Very jolly place—good country to ride over—within reach of the Pitchley."

Heehaw *loquitur* — "Don't do any such thing; you'll find it doosed expensive: they will ask you for £25 for the ball; won't take less than £25 for the hunt, and think you a shabby fellow at that; then they will expect you to ride half a dozen races, or you will be slow. I hear Sir Robert Cliff is there, with fourteen horses, all hunters; your three would be nothing—don't go. The ladies there won't dance with any hunting man that has less than ten horses. Upon my word, I would not advise. I'll tell you a story about Jones Lloyd. Well, he went to Leamington; wanted a little hunting, and dancing, and that kind of thing. Well, he went to the assembly rooms; introduced to doosed nice girl; well, after a time, he said he was going out hunting next day; girl asked him, in a sly kind of way, how many horses he had. What answer do you think he made?—he had four. 'Oh! that isn't enough here,' she said. Would you believe it? She gave him a cold kind of bow next day, and told her friends that he had only four horses to hunt with. Old ladies—the mammas—said he must be a second son, and that they could not let their daughters dance with him any more. A fact, upon my word!" "But I will take a turn at Bath," says the Honourable Lionel. "Bath!!" says Heehaw, in astonishment, as if the Honourable Lionel had spoken of a much hotter place; "they do nothing but play cards there; the old ladies there will clean you out in a month. Very affable, at first, to lead you on. I declare, I believe, some of them must have their cards marked. Don't go on any account whatsoever." "Well, then, I must go to Leicester." "Well, go if you like; you'll be tired of it in a week; all manufacturers there. They talk of yarn, woollens, and such like; they eat with their knife, and pick their teeth with their fork."

But it is at the assembly-room ball that Captain Heehaw, as master of the ceremonies, shines forth in his full effulgence. Talk not to me of Wellington, calm and serene at Waterloo, or of

Edmund Burke, addressing the House of Commons—I state they cannot hold a candle to Heehaw; his noble manner must strike with awe and admiration all beholders. See his stately tread, his scrupulously-brushed whiskers, his smile, his shining boots, the well-padded pigeon-breasted coat and waistcoat, his chapeau, and last, though not least, the blue ribbon across his broad breast. Is it the ribbon of the Order of the Garter? Not at all; it is the emblem of his high office and calling—namely, master of the ceremonies at Cheltenham. Watch him now, as the couples are formed for a quadrille. The orchestra in the gallery will not commence till the wave of the chapeau is given by Heehaw; but they, nevertheless, make sundry tuning noises and scrapings, like horses neighing and impatient to start in a race.

Perhaps I cannot better conclude my description of Captain Heehaw, and how much he values and appreciates the assembly-room balls, than by giving the paragraph which is written by Mr. Charles Dickens, where he would delineate Heehaw's brother M. C. at Bath. It runs thus :—

" 'This is a ball night,' said the M. C., again taking his newly-acquired friend's hand, as he rose to go. 'The ball nights in Bath are moments snatched from Paradise ; rendered bewitching by music, beauty, elegance, fashion, etiquette, and, above all, by the absence of tradespeople, who are quite inconsistent with Paradise, and who have an amalgamation of themselves at the Guildhall every fortnight, which is, to say the least, remarkable — very. Good - bye, good-bye.' And protesting all the way down stairs that he was most satisfied, and most delighted, and overpowered, and flattered, Angelo Cyrus Bantam, Esq., M. C., stepped into a very elegant chariot that waited at the door, and rattled off."

CHAPTER III.

INTRODUCES THE READER TO MY LADY BROADGAUGE; HER HUSBAND IS DIRECTOR OF A RAILWAY; HER HANDSOME RESIDENCE AT ALBERT GATE, HYDE PARK; HER DINNER AND HER GUESTS MENTIONED IN THE MORNING POST; LADY BROADGAUGE'S ANTAGONIST, MRS. SNARLING; LADY B.'S COURT DRESS; MRS. SNARLING'S DITTO; THE WRITER GIVES A SHORT LECTURE TO THE TWO LADIES. THE REV. MR. DOVECOTE, HIS EASTERN TOUR; THE ARAB DONKEY BOYS; THE NEVER-FAIL-TO-BE-FOUND MAN IN THE SHOOTING COAT, WHO TURNS OUT TO BE A "PERFIDIOUS ISLANDER;" THE NATIVE PHYSICIAN'S CURE; "ASSOUAN," THE ASCENT OF THE NILE; ATRA CURA IS IN THE EAST; THE FLEA; MR. THACKERAY'S BUG DISAPPOINTER; A LITTLE GIRL ASKS IF IT BITES; "MISS BADEN;" PAPA IS TAKEN IN AT COLOGNE: MISS PRINCE'S GERMAN IS NOT UNDERSTOOD BY THE GERMANS; MISS BADEN'S BROTHER TOM READS FOR HIS "LITTLE GO;" HE ACTUALLY CUTS UP MAMMA'S BEAUTIFUL PUCE SILK DRESS FOR A RACING JACKET; HIS PAPA DOES NOT LIKE HIM TO FREQUENT THE GAMING TABLES; THE "OULD COW'S HORN;" LADY STIFFNECK ON THE RHINE; LORD STIFFNECK ABUSES THE LANGUAGE, THE DINNERS, THE ROADS, THE MONEY, AND NEARLY EVERYTHING ELSE IN DEUTSCHLAND; TOM'S ULTRA-FRENCH COSTUME. MR. BRIEF, Q. C., IS NEXT INTRODUCED; IS A VERY NOTABLE PERSON; THE TRIAL OF DREDLINCOURT VERSUS DREDLINCOURT; COLONEL SLIGO'S GREAT DEFAMATION OF CHARACTER CASE: THE WIT AND

Lady Broadgauge. [p. 53.

HUMOUR OF MR. BRIEF, Q. C.; MR. BRIEF IS NOT OF A SHY DISPOSITION, NOR DOES HE SPEAK AS IF THE LAST REMAINING BUTTON ON HIS CLOTHES WAS FALLING OFF.

Lady Broadgauge

IS tall and stately in appearance, and seems fully to realise to herself that she is a person of a good deal of importance; not that she would lay much stress on being the wife of a knight, though this is not to be despised, but she knows that she is also the wife of an M. P., and that he has now sat for several Parliaments for Guzzlebury, and that Sir Jonas is also a director of some of the greatest and most important railroads in England. Is not a duke a chairman of one of these lines? and a marquis of another? and is not Sir Jonas intimately acquainted with both of these great people?

Sir Jonas and Lady Broadgauge reside, when in town, at their own house, near Albert-gate, where they give large but select dinner parties, but where I cannot say that the proverb, "In vino veritas," is strictly carried out; besides, Sir Jonas does not speak much on the subject of railways; and it has been found very difficult to draw him out, should he be disinclined that way.

At these dinner parties, there is very often the duke, the chairman of the railway, or the marquis, the chairman of the other; but they are never asked together—no, one of these fine birds is enough at a time. If you take up the *Morning Post* the next day, you will see that " Sir Jonas and Lady Broadgauge entertained at dinner yesterday, at their residence, near Albert-gate, Hyde Park, the Duke of Omnium, Mr. Bagley, M. P.; Sir Lionel and Lady Luttrell; the Solicitor-General, M. P.; Mr. Brief, Q. C.; General Smash, K. C. B., and Lady Smash; Miss Fitz-Arthur; Mrs. Bradshaw, of Lea Park; Miss Baden; the Honourable Arthur Vane, &c. &c.;" and, likely, the paper will add that " in the evening, Sir Jonas and Lady Broadgauge entertained an additional number of their friends." Lady

Broadgauge deserves much credit for her tact in being able to bring together the large railway directors, bankers, &c., and, besides these, a strong muster of that part of the aristocracy who take an interest in such matters.

Lady Broadgauge has an antagonist in the person of Mrs. Snarling, and they have been now, for years, running a kind of neck-and-neck race against each other. Mrs. Snarling is the wife of a wealthy city banker, and it seems as if it had been allotted that these two ladies should be thorns in each other's sides. Does Lady Broadgauge give a dinner party, the next week or so you will see Mrs. Snarling's described also;

does Lady Broadgauge propose to go to Brighton, Mrs. Snarling is likely there before; they both have country-houses in Sussex, where they again come into collision with each other at croquet parties, archery meetings, county assemblies, flower shows, &c., &c. The Sussex county paper will describe how the foliage plants sent in by Mrs. Snarling gained the first prize, and how Lady Broadgauge was second in the same class. How Mr. Hughes, Lady Broadgauge's gardener, deserves great credit for the black grapes sent in for exhibition, and Mr. M'Duff, Mrs. Snarling's gardener, for the green grapes exhibited by him.

The reader is left still in doubt which is the best exhibitor of the two.

Does Lady Broadgauge go to the Queen's drawing-room, you will see her dress described in full, perhaps thus:—

"Train and corsage of very rich vert lumiere silk, beautifully brocaded in silver-lined poult de soie, trimmed tastefully à la grecque with white tulle, spotted in silver; green tulle illusion, silver passementerie, soft white roses, and nœuds of green satin ribbon; corsage trimmed to correspond; petticoat of rich green poult de soie, with bouilloned skirts of green tulle illusion; alternante volants of green tulle, edged green satin and white tulle, beautifully embroidered in silver, studded with soft white roses, and nœuds of green satin ribbon. Head-dress—Diamonds and green velvet, court plume, and silver tulle lappets. Ornaments—Diamonds."

A little further on you will probably find Mrs. Snarling's dress described:—

"Train of richest ruby satin, lined with white gros de Naples, handsomely trimmed with buffons of ruby tulle, rouleaux of satin, and real white Brussels point lace; corsage à la grecque, trimmed to correspond; jupe volants of ruby tulle, with a tunic of real white Brussels point lace, looped up with satin bows; panier and sash for train, trimmed *en suite*. Head-dress—Feathers and lappets. Ornaments—Diamonds and rubies."

Sir Jonas and Lady Broadgauge have no children, therefore Lady Broadgauge is able to devote a great deal of her time to chaperoning young ladies, which she is very fond of doing, especially such a young lady as Miss Baden, who is frequently on a visit with Lady Broadgauge during the London season; but here, again, the two ladies clash, as, whilst Mrs. Snarling has her two daughters to bring out, Lady Broadgauge has Miss Baden or some other young lady to escort, and there is a kind of perpetual bickering going on between them, and innuendos hinted, such as, how heavily the Misses Snarling waltz, whilst Mrs. Snarling hints that she can't bear Miss Baden, with her airs and graces, and her showing off her German, and French, and Italian. Might the writer put in a few words here? To you, Mrs. Snarling, I would more especially address myself, as you are more advanced in the vale of years than your (shall I term her?) antagonist. Why have not you, Mrs. Snarling, more sense than to keep up this endless bickering? or would it not be more honest to throw off the mask, and appear in your true character, as no *wellwisher* (to use a mild term) of Lady Broadgauge? but, instead of this, you smirk, and bow, and shake hands with each other, whilst in your secret hearts you wish each other in Limbo. Alas! alas! must not J. J. N., writer of this brochure, raise his hands and exclaim —What heartlessness! — what sham exists amongst the fashionables of which London Society is composed!

Rev. Mr. Dovecote

Is very chatty about the Eastern tour which he has recently made, in company with a brother clergyman. Marseilles, Alexandria, Suez, Cairo, the Pyramids, the Nile, the Ship Canal, the Cataracts are constantly cropping up in the course of conversation. Besides, the name of Jerusalem, the Holy Sepulchre, the Jordan, Mount of Olives, Jaffa, Beyrout,

The Rev. Mr. Dovecote, as he appeared at the Pyramids. [p. 62.

Mount Lebanon, and the Arabs, with their constant begging for backsheesh (money); how one of the number had the impudence to pick up a common stone of the country, near the Pyramids, and offer to sell it for a " curio" (they speak tolerably good English) ; how they rode on donkeys to the Pyramids, and what a set of precious young ruffians the Arab donkey boys are. They are acquainted with all the English slang, names of Derby winners included, and every bit of scandal going on at home.

For instance, Mr. Dovecote's donkey went by the name of Beautiful for Ever; another was called Mrs. Borrodale ; another John Brown, Captain Snooks,

Billy Barlow, Lord Ranelagh, Not for Joe. Mr. D. observes that romantic ideas are quite driven out of the traveller's mind for the time being by the observation at Alexandria of marine stores, bottled porter shops, &c., and the yelling donkey boys, shrieking, "Ride, sir!" "Donkey, sir!" "Look here, sir," in excellent English. Asinus musters pretty strongly in the East; and though riding a donkey does not seem a very dignified occupation, it is, nevertheless, much practised in the East.

The journey from Jaffa to Jerusalem took about fourteen hours — distance about forty miles; and this was performed by Mr. D. on horseback, on the most wonderful sort of saddle, with fire-shovel stirrups, reins of red worsted, and red padded saddle-cloth, with numerous tags, glass beads, bobtails, &c.

How the never-failing man in the shooting-coat is to be found at Jerusalem, into the pockets of which shooting coat he has his hands dived, and who is pretty easily recognized to be an Englishman; whether he be at Baden or at Paris, whether examining the Pyramids or an Egyptian mummy, whether looking down the crater of Vesuvius or trying the ascent of Mont Blanc, he still carries about him that same defiant calmness of demeanour, and nearly always a certain superciliousness and *gaucherie* of manner, which stamp him as a perfidious islander. Here he is, also, at the Sacred City, and is pushing and elbowing his way to be first in at the door of the Sacred Sepulchre, as he does in his own country at some assembly or concert.

Mr. Dovecote amused Miss Baden by telling the way the people in Syria endeavoured to get cured when ill— after they find the hakum, or native physician, cannot cure them—namely, by sending for the native astrologer, who writes down the name and number of letters in each name of the patient and of his mother, multiplies and divides the sum total, and then, tearing up the paper into very fine shreds, swallows the whole.

Here is, also, another mode of endeavouring to cure a child when sick. The palm leaves distributed on Palm Sunday (which are preserved for such occasions); these are then mixed with olive leaves, salt, and aloes, and the whole then thrown into a brazier of charcoal, and the smoke from this composition constitutes an incense supposed to expel the evil eye. Here, also, Medicus commences his investigation by endeavouring to ascertain from the patient, or from his own calculations, under what star the patient was born.

But to return to Egypt. Mr. Dovecote describes the ascent of the Nile to the first cataract, and the great liability there is, in ascending the Nile, of getting fast on a mud bank, and thereby causing considerable delay; and he describes the number of water-wheels and water-lifts on the banks of the ancient river. The water-wheel in use thousands of years ago still works creakingly beside the river, along which now also stretch the silent telegraph wires. When the party arrived at Assouan, where is the first cataract, how some of the party went in pursuit of crocodiles, and how the Arabs swim down the boiling current of the cataract, for the benefit of the tourist, in the hope of backsheesh; and how a native Arab is never drowned in the boiling, rushing waters ; and how the spectators stand on rocks at the end of the fall, to see the black fellows, who leap in from a ledge one after the other, and are then seen bobbing along and about like the buoys of a net, and are then borne along through the white foam to the feet of the spectators, where they commence a fight for the always expected backsheesh. Mammon appears to rule with considerable power here as elsewhere.

Atra Cura is in the East—you cannot fly from it—in the shape of little skipping animals, and also their brethren of the bite (shall I shock my fair readers' ears? certainly I ought not); but I will mention, to say the least of it, an ingenious contrivance to ward off their attacks. It is thus described:—"You make a sack of calico, big enough for the body, appended to which is a closed chimney of muslin, stretched out by cane hoops, and fastened up to a beam, or against the wall. 'You keep a sharp look out,' says Mr. Thackeray, 'that no flea or bug is on the look out; and, when assured of this, you pop into the bag, tightly closing the orifice after you.' Mr. Thackeray adds:—'This admirable bug-disappointer I tried at Ramlek, and had the only undisturbed night's rest I enjoyed in the East.'"

Reader, there is a little girl belonging to the author, who often sits on papa's knee, and looks at pictures. The usual question, after examining the animal, be it a lion, monkey, parrot, or such like, is, "Does he bite, papa?" If, in the course of our studies, we should come to either of the tormentors before mentioned, especially if supposed to be |Eastern, what a vigorous answer I, J. J. N., will make, when asked, "Does he bite, papa?" "Indeed he does," will be given so forcibly that I fear it will create alarm in the juvenile mind.

Miss Baden.

Miss Baden has, of course, a great deal to say about the Continent, and the best route to it, and how papa could speak French, but no German; and how he went to buy Cologne water at Cologne; and how, after he had got some bottles, he asked the man in the shop if his was the original Eau de Cologne shop, and that he was told most candidly that it was not, but was next door, whereupon *paterfamilias* proceeded to the adjoining shop, and bought some more there also, and afterwards found out that both the shops belonged to the same man; and how, relying on

Miss Baden. [p. 72.

the asseverations of Miss Prince, the governess, who said she could speak German, that papa and mamma took no courier, but they found to their great inconvenience that the natives of Germany did not understand Miss Prince's German, but stared at her, and shook their heads in despair. Miss Baden had, therefore, to interpret. She states that she was most anxious, lately, to sketch the views from the Rhine boat, but it went so fast that she never had time to complete the picture, and at last her indiarubber and pencil fell into the water, and thus put an end to the sketching for that day. Her brother Tom, who was spending his vacation abroad, and also supposed to be reading for his Little-go, was perpetually in one kind of mischief or another. He would come and tell papa that he had found out what he called a dodge, by which he could win at the gaming-table; but papa positively forbade him going near them, and used to wait about with a big stick outside the door of the gambling-house to prevent him entering.

Then Tom must needs ride races at Baden, and actually got hold of mamma's beautiful puce dress (silk), and had it cut up to make a racing-jacket for himself; and then he kept abusing, *in public*, before the inhabitants, all the mineral waters, as either like lucifer matches dissolved in water, or else like rotten eggs and ditch water.

Miss Baden talks of Spa, Schwalbach, Cologne, Ems, Bonn, Wiesbaden, Brussels, Aix la Chapelle, Geneva, Vevay, Paris, Tours, Dieppe, the Rigi; and how, as the reader is no doubt aware, the people sleep on the summit, to be in time to see the sun rise; and how the sleepers are aroused by the ranz des vache in the morning, a little before Phœbus Apollo begins to show his face; and how a bard of Erin, no doubt somewhat nettled at being roused from his slumbers, wrote these very remarkable lines in the visitors' book:—"Views and sunrise anything but satisfactory, attendance middling, dietary middling;" and then, in a moment of poetic inspiration, he added :—

"The divil such music, since I was born,
Did I ever hear like the ould cow's horn."¹

Then Miss Baden describes how some people are always downstairs in the cabin—nay, even reading the *Times* newspaper or *Galignani*, whilst passing the most beautiful parts of the Rhine. You will, no doubt, often see such as my Lady Stiffneck, in her travelling carriage, looking cross and hot, whilst her

---

¹ The reader will remember that a horn is really blown to rouse people up to view the sun rise.

daughter sits languidly, reading or knitting. Yes, there they are, taking no more interest in the view than if they were passing the flattest and ugliest parts of the Shannon. Lord Stiffneck himself I am not so much surprised about, as he has come abroad to oblige his wife, but has never ceased railing at the language, the heat, the dinners, the roads, and the money, since he has put his foot in Deutschland.

I must admit that it seems absurd for people to come to the Continent if they do not intend to put up with some little trouble. Why should we English be continually growling whilst abroad, and yet when we get home very many of us commence bragging of all we have seen? Miss Baden talks a great deal about Biarritz, the French watering-place—and how pleasant the bathing is there—and how blue the sea is—and as the water is quite tepid, how people remain in for hours, where they walk, talk, and swim, or float by the aid of gourds—and how all the bathers are dressed in the costume des Bains—and, O! mirabile dictu, there is a swimming master (for the Prince Imperial), who is *decoré*, who (what will the world come to?) teaches the ladies to swim.

But to return to Tom, Miss Baden's brother. His costume would amuse most people to see—viz., a pair of wide peg-top trousers; white jean boots, with shiny tips to them; a waistcoat cut à la Francaise; wristbands of shirt turned up; his hair cropped short, especially at the back of the head; the head itself ornamented with a white hat, with the nap about two inches long, and as if brushed the wrong way; the truth is, Mr. Tom adopted this ultra-French costume for a lark. Reader, we will now, for the present, bid Tom farewell, and we trust that he will pass his Little-go (which papa and mamma are very anxious he should do); but I fear there are very great doubts about his success. What, then, will be the difficulty of the Great, if the Little-go is so big to poor Tom?

Mr. Brief, Q. C.

Mr. Brief is, as I need scarcely say, a very eminent member of the legal profession. He was retained in that recent case, Dredlincourt *versus* Dredlincourt, which created so much sensation in all circles of society. The Right Honourable the Solicitor-General, M. P.; Serjeant Rebutter; Mr. Windyman, Q. C.; Mr. Bagley, Q. C.; and Mr. Meales, of the Outer Bar, were all, including Mr. Brief, Q. C., retained in the case. It was a trial about title, and Mr. Brief discovered the weak point in the case—viz., the so-called Scotch marriage years back; and brought the illegality to bear so much against the defendant, that he gained the lawsuit through his perseverance and ingenuity, and henceforth Mr. Brief, Q. C., was a man of mark, and no more rising man in his profession. Barristers spoke to each other—Brief will get into Parliament next general election ; Brief will be made a Right Honourable ; Brief will be the next Solicitor-General ; he will be one of the best speakers they ever had in the House ; what a splendid prospect before him !

I must give some extracts from a recent case to show Mr. Brief's wit and legal acumen. The case, if I remember rightly, was between Colonel Sligo, the proprietor of a newspaper at Portsmouth, and Philip Moore, the owner of a public-house in the same town.

The Bear and Bacchus was much frequented by soldiers and others, and the military authorities became so much impressed with the belief that it was not desirable that soldiers should frequent the above-named public house, that they issued an order that no soldiers in Portsmouth garrison, or any soldiers whatever, should go to the aforesaid Bear and Bacchus.

This was mentioned in the Portsmouth paper, of which Colonel Sligo is the proprietor, under the head of military news. Thus:—

"An order has been issued by the authorities in this garrison, that no soldier will be permitted to enter the public-house called the Bear and Bacchus, situated in Barrack-street, in this town."

The damages were laid at £1000.

Mr. Boshley, Q. C., briefly stated the case for the plaintiff. His client was a trader, carrying on business in Barrack-street, and complained that the paragraph published in the Portsmouth paper had seriously injured his client in his trade and calling, and he further averred that his client's business had fallen off to the extent of £30 a week, an injury of a serious character had been done his (Mr. Boshley's) client, and if the jury awarded him pecuniary compensation for that injury, such compensation would be just to him.

The plaintiff, Philip Moore, was then examined, and stated that the alleged libel was injurious to his business; he did not keep a disorderly house, and, on a recent occasion, when a Fenian song was sung by two civilians and a soldier, he turned them out of his house.

Mr. Brief, Q. C., cross-examined witness. His house was situated in the street directly leading to the barracks. It was like a mousetrap to catch the soldiers as they came out [laughter]. I know an attorney named Fitzhenry.

Did you direct him to write a letter to Colonel Sligo?

Answer — He read me a letter over the counter about it, but I never authorized him.

Did that letter say you wanted damages for injury and loss sustained in consequence of an improper and unauthorized notice being taken of your place of business, and asking to be favoured with the name of Colonel Sligo's attorney?

Answer—Yes, I remember Fitzhenry reading that over the counter to me.

And you heard the most proper reply that was sent him by Colonel Sligo?

"PORTSMOUTH GAZETTE OFFICE,
February 17*th*, 1868.

"SIR—I have the honour to acknowledge the receipt of your letter of the 16th instant, and, in reply, beg to state, that my attorneys are Messrs. Scrouge, of this town, who will receive and act on any communication you may desire to send them.

"With reference to the paragraph you allude to, and which I had not observed until the receipt of your letter to-day, it was evidently taken from Garrison Orders of the 10th of December last.

"Paragraphs of a similar kind have constantly been published. No one knows better than yourself and your client that the 'Portsmouth Gazette' published that paragraph without any intention to injure Mr. Philip Moore, and that it would have readily published any explanation that you and he desired, had such a request been made.

"As you prefer to adopt another course, the matter can go to a jury, with whose decision I am quite satisfied to abide.

"Your obedient Servant,
"ARTHUR E. SLIGO."

Christopher Egan, journeyman tailor, examined, and deposed that he occasionally PATRONIZED plaintiff's house, by going in and purchasing liquor there. He withdrew his custom because the trade to which he belonged required that he should not deal exclusively in one place.

MR. BRIEF, Q. C.—I suppose you wished to have free range of all the public-houses in the town of Portsmouth [laughter].

John Egan, another tailor, said he heard something was published in the "Portsmouth Gazette" respecting the house; he felt DELICATE [laughter] about going into it after that.

John Burne deposed that he was in the habit of occasionally getting a bottle of ginger beer in the plaintiff's house, and that he had lately discontinued doing so. He could not assign any reason for ceasing to go there, as he was altogether in the dark on the subject.

Mr. Brief, Q. C., stated the case for the defendant in an extremely able speech. The defendant, Colonel Sligo, they had been told by Mr. Boshley, was the proprietor of a highly-respectable and influential paper. The respectability of the journal and respectability of its proprietor had been brought before the jury as an argument why they should deal heavily in point of damages in this case; but was a man to be victimized in a court of justice because he had a high character? He (Mr. Brief) had no wish, in any degree, to asperse the character of the plaintiff, who carried on the trade of a publican in a neighbourhood where there were a great many in the same trade as himself. The publicans were nearly as numerous about Portsmouth, Gosport, and neighbourhood, as the lawyers in Westminster Hall, and that was saying a deal for them [laughter]. The plaintiff was not long in business, and as long as his ale was sound and his groceries fresh, he was doing a thriving trade. The position of his house was good, being exactly in full view of the barracks, so that when a soldier came out for his daily walk, and to spend the few pence which a grateful country enabled him to do, the plaintiff was the first to receive him— there he was in the position of the spider treating the soldier as the fly. His house was occasionally visited by soldiers; but the military authorities, for some reasons best known to themselves, thought proper to prohibit soldiers entering that house. The prohibition was in the Garrison Orders of the 10th of December last, and was then published in the "Portsmouth Gazette." But it was not until February that the plaintiff thought proper to make any complaint about it. Colonel Sligo never heard anything of it till he received Fitzhenry's letter, which the Colonel answered in a straightforward manner. If the plaintiff had then thought himself aggrieved, and desired an explanation, the columns of the "Portsmouth Gazette" were open to afford him every opportunity of giving it publicity. Nothing further was heard of the proceedings until, on the 8th of April (it was a pity it was not on the first of that month), a summons and plaint was served, and the case was now attempted to be propped up by rubbishy evidence. Rubbish had the advantage that it could be used for filling up holes; but the only purpose that could be served by the production of the fellows produced on the other side was to make holes in the plaintiff's case [laughter]. Nothing takes place in the matter until the plaintiff's woes reach the ear of Peter Fitzhenry, who bears an apostolic name, and resides in Upper Wellington-street. On hearing them, his forensic heart is overcome; and, inspired by the purest and most philanthropic motives, he resolves to vindicate the wrongs of the plaintiff, although uninvited by Mr. Moore to do so. The jury should know that some of the attorneys have aides-de-camp, gentlemen attached to their staff, who, like officers of the staff at a review, ride across the field like grim death, at the bidding of the Commander-in-Chief, to tell one regiment to fire a blank discharge at another [laughter]. In like manner, the aides-de-camp attached to the staff of an attorney are out looking for actions. If a cause of action is simmering, one of these gentlemen will soon be found to blow it into a blaze. Accordingly, Fitzhenry hears of the case, and, without authority, he writes a letter to the defendant, demanding satisfaction, commencing his letter "Chambers," "Camera obscura" [laughter]. That is always the way they began. On the top of his letter the royal arms. Where did Peter Fitzhenry get that note paper? At all events, it had upon it the royal arms, with the Lion and Unicorn standing on their hind-legs, fighting, he supposed, for the possession of Colonel Sligo's purse [laughter]. When Philip Moore heard of it, he said he was not quite sure if he would go on with the action. Fitzhenry's letter produced a reply from Colonel Sligo, and a fairer letter never was written, penned, without legal assistance of any kind, from the dictates of his heart; but nothing more was heard of the matter until Mr. James Garrett, the present attorney upon the record, appeared upon the scene, and he produced the witnesses they had that day to sustain

Mr. Garrett (a skilful attorney) carefully turning over old women in neighbourhood of Barrack-street, in order to try to sustain a libel (Colonel Sligo *versus* Philip Moore). [p. 94.

the libel, and get £1000 damages. Mr. Garrett was a skilful attorney, and he (Mr. Brief) felt sure there was not an old woman in the neighbourhood of Barrack-street whom he did not carefully turn over and cross-examine, to see if it could assist in any way to sustain the case [laughter]. Owing to the manner in which the summons and plaint was issued, and innuendos put upon the words, the defendant was excluded from pleading in justification that the publication was true; that the order was issued, and that the military were strictly prohibited from resorting to the plaintiff's house. The meaning of the paragraph was distorted, and he denied that it bore the interpretation put upon it by the plaintiff. The "Portsmouth Gazette" was a newspaper whose boast and pride was that it catered for the information of every class of the community. There was information for the ladies, for the gentlemen, the clergy, and for the laity, the lawyers, and the doctors; then there was information for the military, and for that large and important section of the female community who took an interest in the affairs of the army. Amongst other military items published was the matter complained of. The learned counsel proceeded to comment on the alleged libel, and concluded a very able speech by submitting that the case was one of the most absurd and frivolous ever brought into a court of justice.

Lieut.-Colonel Evans, Town Major, was examined, and produced the book containing garrison orders. The paragraph complained of was a copy from those orders, and, in his opinion, did not bear the interpretation put upon it by the plaintiff.

Mr. Baron Stairleigh charged the jury, briefly recapitulating the facts of the case, and explaining the law bearing upon it.

The jury then retired; in an hour they came into court. The Foreman stated there was no possibility of agreeing to a verdict; there were eleven for finding for the defendant, and one for the plaintiff.

Baron Stairleigh directed them to retire again, in the hope they might agree: the question was a simple one.

In a short time the jury again came into court.

The Foreman stated it was impossible they could agree; there were eleven for the defendant.

Another Juror—There are some people, my lord, who will not listen to reason.

Baron Stairleigh directed the jury to be discharged.

Some persons speak in public as if they were labouring under this difficulty, that there is, so to speak, a certain button connected with their entire clothing which, if once disengaged from its fastening, will bring down all their apparel in one fell slip; that the hearers are intently gazing at this button, which it is only too evident to all, and especially to the speaker himself, is manifestly slipping away by degrees from its frail hold. Alas! how is it possible that the average Englishman could speak under (to say the least of it) such very *disagreeable* circumstances?

If this is the case with most Englishmen, it certainly is not so with Mr. Brief, Q. C., who has not any diffidence of this sort about him, but the button is, so to speak, fast and firm.

CHAPTER IV.

MISS FANNY SMILES: NOT MUCH WILL BE SAID ABOUT HER BECAUSE —— MAJOR GOLUMPUS IS NEXT INTRODUCED. HIS FONDNESS FOR GOOD FARE, HIS GREAT EXPLOIT IN INDIA, ABOUT WHICH THE MAJOR DRAWS THE "LONG BOW;" THE MAJOR'S RECIPE FOR A SALAD. YOUNG DE BOOTS TRYING TO ARGUE WITH THE MAJOR ABOUT THE QUALITY OF THE WINE. MRS. WHITMORE, CALLED ALSO MRS. WRITEMORE—MESSRS. SOFTSAWDER AND DIDDLE ARE HER PUBLISHERS; HER NOVEL CALLED "THE DUCHESS;" HER POETIC EFFUSIONS, "ODE TO A ROUGE POT," ETC. THE BOOK IS SOLD AT "THE LADIES' BABIES' BIB-AND-TUCKER BAZAAR." THE BIRMINGHAM CHICKEN GETS A COPY OF THE BOOK OF POETRY, WHICH HE KEEPS IN HIS BACK PARLOUR. SIR JONAS BROADGAUGE; IS A DIRECTOR OF THE GREAT NORTH AND SOUTH JUNCTION RAILWAY; DOES NOT SPEAK MUCH ABOUT SHARES AT DINNER PARTIES; THE CHELSEA CHAIN PIER TRIAL; THE BRIDGE IS FLAT, THE SHARES ARE FLATTER, THE SHAREHOLDERS FLATTEST OF ALL; SIR JONAS BROADGAUGE'S PORTRAIT, AS SEEN AT THE ROYAL ACADEMY EXHIBITION.

MISS FANNY SMILES is the next in order as we pass round the table; but I do not purpose detaining my reader long under this heading, as I must hurry on towards the completion of the description of the guests at table. Suffice it to say, that the young lady in question is of very prepossessing appearance, and pleasing manners; that Miss Smiles and her sisters are both chaperoned by Mrs. Whitmore, of whom more anon. Perhaps I may mention that Miss F. S. is so much admired that she has had many opportunities of changing her name, should she have wished it. I, indeed, for one, have always been an admirer of the young lady in question, —— but I must stop here, as I may commit myself in print, which would not do (as our friends in Hibernia say) "at all, at all."

Ah! Miss S., how many more hearts are you going to break before you finally decide who is to be the happy individual? Answer me that question, I desire of you. *Fare thee well!*

Major Golumpus.

"Then, pledge the Boar, the mighty Boar!
Fill high the cup with me;
Here's luck to all who fear no fall
When next the Boar they see."
Indian Hunting Song.

Talks of his exploits in India, where he was in action, and commanded a regiment of irregular cavalry, and what signal service he performed during the late Indian mutiny; also the Major describes his exploits, lion hunting, also elephant, and hog hunting. The Major, who is a bit of a gourmet, has been lately praising Mrs. Jones' turbot, and then, turning to Mr. Jones, he says—

"This is very nice champagne, Jones; I don't think I ever tasted better."

"Glad you like it," says Jones. "Major, try another glass with me." And down goes No. 2 glass.

Ah! Major, towards the end of the evening you will be telling some of your astonishing tales, as wonderful nearly as those of the renowned Major Goliah Gahagan, late of the East India Company's service.

The men ask a new comer to Cheltenham, Did you ever hear the Major tell the story of all the men he killed in India? Before dinner it is 2 in number; after the ladies have left the table they number 3; and it has been said that the Major, still later in the evening, at the club, has stated there were 4.

But the most surprising part of the matter is, that these individuals—call them by the numerals 2, 3, or 4, as you will—were, according to the gallant Major's account, all killed at once. Yes, reader, by a single swoop of his victorious sword. It might, in truth, have these words engraved upon it—

"Sheath me not without honour."

His friends who were near him in action say he really killed 2, and they account for the number 4 by saying that the Major must then, or shortly afterwards, have seen double, which would account for the numeral 4, instead of the numeral 2 ; and thus, as we used to say when in College, *Q. E. D.*, or *quod erat demonstrandum*. The subject has now become a monomania of the Major's ; some are affected with a monomania one way, some another. For instance, a sporting friend of the writer (Jack Litton), who backed Springy Jack heavily for the Derby, thinks Springy should have won, and that he was a better horse than Surplice. Now all the world knows that such is not the case, and that the best horse of the two won.

The late Lord Aldborough appears to have had a monomania that Professor Holloway had cured him of some inveterate disease. This is a monomania of a different class to the first-mentioned.

The writer knew a young officer in a light cavalry regiment who had a monomania for sticks and whips, and he had collected together such a number, of all sizes and shapes, that they could be numbered up to tens of scores. This was a very peculiar monomania.

Some men, again, have a monomania in this way, that they think they are ill, or near dying. The writer knew a baronet many years ago—he is now deceased—who led a most regular life, as to dietary, sleep, &c., and appeared in good health, and yet he would get into a huff if you hinted he was looking well, but if you said that he did not appear well, it was the most sure plan to adopt to put him in a good humour, and to get him to think well of you; in fact, like a character described in one of Captain Marryatt's novels, he never was happy unless he was confoundedly miserable.

The Major gives little dinners of the most recherché kind; number of guests consisting of three or four usually. Everything that is brought to table being first-class, his invitation to dinner is much sought after in Cheltenham; indeed, when a man gets the credit for giving first-rate champagne, moselle, claret, and port, he may be sure of always finding plenty to share it with him.

I cannot help comparing my friend Major Pompous's dinners with those of Major Golumpus. Pompous, between ourselves my reader, is inclined to brag a good bit. "Come down, my boy," said he, at the Philadelphos Club, "and have a day with the Duke's hounds. There is an excellent country to ride over, and I'll give you as good a bottle of claret or old port as you ever drank in your life." This invitation having been given on several occasions, I lately availed myself of it. The hunting and country were good enough, so I will pass this by; but the much-talked-of wine did not turn out at all according to expectations. The sherry, if not Marsala, was very much on a par with that article, and the port wine was—Bah! a confounded piece of deception. The Major did not brag about it much, as he did at the Club, but it was laid on the table, and in sooth was not troubled by either of us much. The Major said, as the evening was wet, he would try some hot punch, and I was therefore left to make what acquaintance I wished with the port wine, which was not a long one. The truth is, I suspect that Mrs. Major Pompous has a good deal more control in the house and cellar than Pompous, and that she did not on this occasion bring out the port with the pet seal on it; Pompous and Mrs. P. having had a slight row the day before about some excursion to London to see the Opera, and a two months' excursion on the Continent. But enough of these little secrets. If our other Major brags less, he is more certain in quality of supply. So hurrah for our Major Golumpus, and long life to him, or, as they say in Erin, "More power to him."

But, to return to Major G., who, as

we have said before, is a gourmet, not a gourmand: the difference between the two a writer states to be this—" A gourmet is the man who selects for his nice and learned delectation the most choice delicacies prepared in a scientific manner; whilst, on the other hand, the gourmand bears a near analogy to that class of eaters (ill-naturedly, let us suppose) denominated or classed with Aldermen."

I would here remark how absurd it is of that conceited fellow, young De Boots, who has passed a couple of terms at Oxford, to set up to be a judge of wine against our old connoisseur, Major G. Why, I have it from the best authority (that is, from a schoolfellow of De Boots) that he was flogged soundly three halfs ago, for not translating "Horatius Flaccus" into decent English, rendering "Simplex Munditiis" "A simple fellow in the World;" and yet here he is now in Cheltenham, trying to argue with the Major about the quality of ports and clarets, trying to look knowing as he examines the cork after drawing, and closes one eye to see the colour and beeswing of the port. Why, the Major was a judge of wine before he was drinking his mother's milk.

The Major talks with a good deal of gusto of the dinners he has had at the Trois Freres Provenceaux, the Rocher

Cancale, and in London, at the Trafalgar, Greenwich, and the Traveller's Club, at the Star and Garter, Richmond, the Oriental Club, and at Brookes' and the Reform.

The Major has a particular recipe for a sauce for wild-fowl, which he manufactures apart, but as far as the writer can ascertain it is made thus—

    1 salt-spoon of salt.
    $\frac{1}{2}$ to $\frac{3}{4}$ of cayenne.
    1 dessert-spoon lemon juice.
    1   ,,   pounded sugar.
    1   ,,   ketchup.
    2   ,,   Harvey.
    3   ,,   port wine.

To be well mixed and heated, and then poured over the bird.

Then he prides himself on the concoction of a salad, which is nearly the same as that recommended by the late Sydney Smith.

I give here the latter gentleman's advice, on the principle, that a good thing cannot be too often repeated; and, indeed, the Major himself highly extols the salad thus made.

Recipe for a winter salad, by the late Rev. Sydney Smith.

"Two large potatoes, passed through kitchen sieve,
 Unwonted softness to the salad give.
 Of mordant mustard add a single spoon;
 Distrust the condiment which bites so soon;
 But deem it not, thou man of herbs, a fault,
 To add a double quantity of salt.
 Three times the spoon with oil of Lucca crown,
 And once with vinegar procured from town.

True flavour needs it, and your poet begs
The pounded yellow of two well-boiled eggs.
Let onion atoms lurk within the bowl,
And, scarce suspected, animate the whole;
And, lastly, on the flavoured compound toss
A magic teaspoon of anchovy sauce.
Then, though green turtle fail, though venison's tough,
And ham and turkey are not boiled enough,
Serenely full, the epicure may say—
Fate cannot harm me—I have dined to-day!"

The Major's year is spent somewhat thus:—

In the winter, hunting, &c.

In summer, some four months in London, then a moor in Scotland, or a run on the Continent, or, perhaps, a stay in Paris for two months, then back again to Cheltenham for the winter,—a pleasant life enough, each place being taken somewhat at its prime.

The Major has had a considerable number of servants during my acquaintance with him. Stratford was Brush's predecessor, and a very good servant he was till he began that confounded betting on races (he would wish to take me into his confidence) and used to say, that in a day or two he would get the name of the horse to back for Chester Cup, Derby, Leger, or some such race, but the writer declined the proffered service, and the rapid means pointed out to make a fortune; as I concluded, if the fortune could be so easily made, that the adviser of the tip would be the first to avail himself of this information. Stratford and his master parted company in London, the former having sent in a bill of £30 for eggs and butter consumed by the Major during his stay of two months in the metropolis. I have little doubt that Stratford went to the Wheel of Fortune public-house, where the servants' club is held, and *descanted* on the severe master that Major Golumpus turned out. Brush, of course, as the new servant was put in full possession of all the Major's peculiarities, &c.

Stratford had a most wonderful varnish, a recipe of his own, and, in sooth during the London season to see the

Major turn out for the park, and see his *tout ensemble*, commencing with the well-brushed hat, down to the Stratfordian varnished boots, was a sight for the gods to behold.

Mrs. Whitmore.

> Our lips in derision we curl
> Unless we are told how a Duchess
> Conversed with her cousin the Earl.

Nicknamed Mrs. *Writemore* by her acquaintances. Heaven bless us! why she has already written some 25 novels, besides essays, reviews, desultory thoughts, recollections of travels, memoirs, articles for magazines, and poetry. Write more, indeed! to be sure she will—

> " Tours, travels, essays, too, I wist,
> And novels to thy mill bring grist."

Mrs. Whitmore, an authoress.

Mrs. Whitmore's pen slips along with such wonderful rapidity and grace, her specially-found critics take care to puff her well. About Christmas time we often read a notice, which runs somewhat to this effect:—

"We are given to understand, that Messrs. Softsawder and Diddle, the well-known enterprising publishers, are about to publish a new work, from the pen of the well-known authoress, Mrs. Whitmore, authoress of 'Alonzo,' 'Castle Forward,' 'The Duchess,' &c., &c. We are at a loss which to admire most—the vigorous compass of the authoress' mind, or the exquisite fairy-like delicacy of the same. We are permitted to say here, that this new work of the fair authoress is, in the opinion of many eminent literary men, far in advance of anything she has previously written; and it may be added, that the public mind has been (so to speak) quite on the tip-toe of expectation since the *on dit* has been circulated that this new work was in the press."

Thus does Mrs. Whitmore get her novel announced, and when published it will be dandled and fondled into further notice.

We would now call the reader's attention to Mrs. Whitmore's writings in prose; and then examine, in a somewhat cursory manner, her poetic inspirations.

And first we would call attention to "The Duchess," as a specimen of the first-named class of writing.

In most of Mrs. Whitmore's novels, but especially in the one called "The Duchess," we are introduced into such high life, that at last the reader begins to turn up his nose at a mere Baron or Baronet.

Mrs. Whitmore does not do things by halves; but gives us the manners and ways of the *élite* of the nobility. We learn the thoughts and mode of living of Dukes and Marquises, Duchesses and Marchionesses, celebrated statesmen, wits, and beaux. Perhaps it is on account of Mrs. Whitmore taking so high a flight, that the cause is discovered why "The Duchess" sells so well; as people who are not made of so fine a clay, and approach more to the delph of society, are able, by paying their guinea to the circulating library—are able as it were, I repeat, to enter the stately mansions, beautiful parks, elegant town residences, boudoirs, and drawing-rooms, of the aforesaid Duchesses, Dukes, Marchionesses, &c.

Nay, the reader feels as if he had a Duke by the arm, and was walking down Pall Mall with him, on such a delightful footing of familiarity does one feel with these exalted personages.

Mrs. Whitmore's novels are much

read at sea-side watering places, where you may see young ladies perched on rocks, with parasols over their heads, and uglies on their bonnets, perusing, during the long summer's day, these delightful productions.

I myself have often come across these fair readers in Mr. Mugford's library at Brightstone, or other sea-side watering places, where they come hastily in to ask for the second volume or third volume of "The Duchess." Mugford's reply is very often that "it is in hands; but I will send the volume as soon as I get it back. Will you take 'Mrs. Montague Jones' Dinner Party,' or some other work, instead?"

There is a peculiarity in Mrs. Whitmore's writings (and I think it will be found prevalent amongst fashionable novels), namely, the somewhat plentiful sprinkling of French words and idioms through the work. It appears quite remarkable how the Duchesses, whilst they languidly recline on the sofa, feel such a difficulty in expressing, in their own language, their own thoughts, but must have recourse to the French language to give these thoughts utterance.

For instance in the first fifteen pages of "The Duchess," I find the following French words and idioms:—protegè, par excellence, mon cher, nouveau riche, mesalliance, parvenu, eclat, juste ciel, besides some others.

>   —" gentle Sir, I've brought
> The midnight harvest of much toil and thought."—
> " A novel ?"—"just three volumes when in print."
> "The title, ma'am ? what taking chapters in't ?"
> "The characters are all from life you'll find ;
> I've ta'en a precious peep the scenes behind,
> Broad hints that cannot fail to raise the dust,
> A parry here, and there a desp'rate thrust ;
> Three Lords unmasked, a DUCHESS to the life."
>   MONTGOMERY.

Nor is the perusal of Mrs. Whitmore's novels confined to the upper and middle ranks, but,

> " E'en sluttish housemaids crib a farthing light,
>   To whimper o'er the novel's page by night."
>   IBID.

We will now, with the reader's permission, glance at Mrs. Whitmore's poetical effusions. In the beautiful volume of poems published by Softsawder and Diddle, I find the following effusions amongst many others:—

"A shriek from Erin."

"The hunting morn."

"Lines to a pig (guinea)."

"Address to a faded bouquet."

"Ode to a dead canary bird."

"Address to a rouge pot."

In the impassioned poem to the canary bird, the authoress describes how the bird began to decline in health [could he have had the pip?], then he refused his accustomed sugar and seeds, then in a very touching manner she describes his faded plumage [I believe I required the use of a pocket-handkerchief whilst reading this portion especially of the poem], at last his gasping for breath, and then his final kick. The authoress concludes with a soliloquy, that it may have been better to die thus than fall into the hands [I beg pardon, reader], the claws of the cat, as not a vestige would remain in the one case, whilst in the other, his remains can be transferred to the bird-stuffer to exercise his art upon, and his form would still be preserved and cherished by his fond mistress: this appears to the fair authoress to be her sole consolation for the loss of her bird.

I have been frequently pressed to buy the Book of Poetry at bazaars, &c. I remember at the bazaar for the "Ladies' Babies' Bib and Tucker General Loan Fund," that Captain Dash, and young De Boots, bought a volume each from the Miss Languishs; the volumes were gorgeous in crimson and gold. The Captain, when asked to buy the book, answered somewhat thus: "Poetry, eh? well I don't think I am up to that sort of thing, eh! De Boots? but I will buy it when you urge me" [here he gave a killing look, as he thought, at Miss Languish]. When the book arrived at the Captain's lodgings his landlady thus expressed herself, " O Lawks ! what a 'ansom book, well I never." The word handsome must have applied to the outside only, as Mrs. Rattles, the Captain's landlady, had not as yet read a line of the poetry, or had shed tears over the defunct canary bird-story.

I am given to understand that the book afterwards passed into the possession of Captain Dash's washerwoman, "Mrs. O'Leary," who purloined it from its rightful owner, and she will, I have no doubt, get it exchanged into gin, or her native whiskey, at an early opportunity.

Alas, how are the mighty fallen, when this beautiful book of poems should be found in the possession of an Irish washerwoman, and then exchanged at the Pawnbroker's into money to buy ardent spirits.

As far as I have been able to trace the fate of the book young De Boots bought, I can only learn this much, that it is now ornamenting the back-parlour shelf of the "Cat and Bagpipes" public-house in Birmingham, and that the Landlady of the house, who is also the wife of the "Birmingham Bruiser," lays great store upon it, I suppose for its cheerful and pleasant-looking binding.

Sir Jonas Broadgauge.

O Cornwall! happy, blest spot of ground,
Where richest ores of every kind abound;
Thy very hills are brass, thy rocks are tin;
Thy wealth is not exposed without, but hid within.
Cornish Bard.

Is somewhat stout in person, and of florid complexion; when he walks you hear a peculiar kind of creak in the boots that often belong to the monied class. Not that the creak is loud, oh, no! it is soft and euphonious; it is a gentle sort of creak, which gives importance to Sir Jonas Broadgauge's walk across the Board-room. When Sir J. B. was a merchant, this creak used to strike awe into the clerks employed by Sir Jonas; and as the noise increased, as the originator of the noise ascended the stairs, any light conversation was laid aside, and all was "*hushed and still as summer's eve,*" save the noise occasioned by the scribbling of pens.

In costume Sir Jonas adopts a kind of dress which is seen amongst bankers of the old school: a coat cut according to the old style of fashion of some 50 years ago—(he still resembles some of the merchants of that date.) He wears no such thing, for instance, as a turned down collar, but has a cravat going twice round the neck, such as was the old style of wear. In fact, everything in the matter of dress about Sir Jonas is good, massive, quiet, and business-like, eradicating all idea in the beholder's mind of any resemblance to the modern fop. Sir Jonas wears gaiters, which, however, are in good character with the rest of his costume; added to this, an eye-glass dangles from his neck, or is thrust into a side-pocket in his waistcoat. So much for his dress. In appearance Sir Jonas has a bland sort of aspect generally on his countenance, and is capable of assuming the utmost suavity of manner; he is not excitable, but is cool and collected on all occasions, and is, therefore, the better able to bear much fatigue. He is considered in the House of Commons a man of authority on railway matters, and on monetary affairs also, though he is not, strictly speaking, a financier, having given his attention more to the subject of railways, foreign loans, &c., and, moreover, has succeeded in making money.

It has been said, that out of every 100 men you meet in the city, 99 out of these are trying to make money or a fortune, and that only 5 per cent. make the fortune. Though there are so few in the hundred that succeed, we must put Sir Jonas in the fortunate category.

I suppose, reader, I had better give here Sir J. B.'s antecedents, that is, as far as I am acquainted with them.

Sir Jonas was originally a merchant on the East Coast, but having failed, he has, by the advice of his brother (a stockbroker), taken up his present course of life; and this brother has been of great service to him, as he puts Sir Jonas up to what is termed a good thing; and the brother, on the other hand, is equally able to serve the stockbroker, by allowing his name to be attached to prospectuses of various companies; in point of fact, they understand each other perfectly as to their respective duties toward each other.

Added to this, Sir Jonas understands the true secret of successful speculation, as he is instructed when, not only to buy to advantage, but when to sell to advantage also.

I must not omit to mention that Sir Jonas is a shareholder and director of the Universal Banking Company. This company brought forward several schemes some few years back, which did not turn out successes. I will mention two of the most prominent—viz., "The Extraction of Sunbeams from Cucumbers Company," and "The Sawdust Bread Company."

An ingenious chemist invented the first-mentioned plan; and, as the prospectus stated, the sunbeams would be carefully bottled, and then used for heating our rooms. Even on the most gloomy day in winter, we could let loose the bottled sunbeams, and thus we could enjoy all the advantages of a fine day indoors, though out of doors it might be raining, or freezing, or sleeting. It turned out afterwards, that the sunbeams refused to enter the bottles, use whatever persuasion they could to get them to do so. Hence the failure of the company.

Sir Jonas Broadgage afterwards brought out a very able pamphlet, in which he reviewed his past connexion with the bank; and showed how that the schemes in which the bank was connected—namely, the Bread Company, and the Sunbeams from Cucumbers

Company—appeared to him, as well as others he is acquainted with, as a very plausible undertaking; but, unfortunately, he had been mistaken. This was all the explanation given to the unfortunate shareholders.

En passant. How is it, dear reader, that if a man plays at cards, and loses all his money, or goes to the gambling table and gets rid of it all there, there is little or no sympathy shown for him; but if he goes on the stock exchange and rids himself of his money, he is held up to the world as a man that has been unfortunate in speculation, and is an object of pity rather than censure?

But to return to Sir Jonas Broadgauge.

"A surprising man is Sir Jonas." These remarkable words were addressed to me lately by a bank clerk in the Universal Bank, and indeed there appears much truth in the remark; as, after the unhappy denouement of the unfortunate companies—viz., The Sunbeams from Cucumbers, and The Sawdust Bread, it does seem SURPRISING that we should have been honoured with several long letters published in the newspapers, showing up again Sir B.'s connexion with these companies. Time was, when if people misconducted an affair, they tried to hide their misdeeds. "Mais nous avons changé tout cela." We are now favoured with public letters, tend-ing only to show, as far as the writer can discern, how gullable the British public still continue to be, and how roguish directors frequently are in practice. Sir Jonas heads his letter with the well-known passage "'*Tis not in mortals to command success.*"

I think we may, in truth, agree with the clerk aforesaid, and exclaim with him, that Sir Jonas Broadgauge *is* a surprising man.

At a recent trial the following questions were put to Sir Jonas Broadgauge:—

MR. BOSHLEY, Q. C.—I believe, Sir Jonas, you are a director of several railways, and of the Chelsea Chain Pier Company?

Answer.—I am.

Question.—Are you aware that the shares of the Chain Pier Company were not all allotted?

Answer.—I am aware of it.

Question.—Do you know what the capital of the Company was to be, as announced in the prospectus?

Answer.—£25,000.

Question.—And what was subscribed?

Answer.—About £5000.

Question.—How was the capital expended, I mean the £5000?

SIR JONAS, looking to the Judge—My Lord, am I compelled to answer this question in full, as it may militate against the company should a new one be formed, as I have no doubt there will?

JUDGE.—You must answer the question.

SIR JONAS.—Well then, as far as I am aware, there was a certain sum given to a certain stockbroker, amounting to £1000, for floating the company, and extra expenses.

Question.—Who was the stockbroker?

Answer.—I have understood that my brother was employed, and paid by the company.

MR. BOSHLEY, Q. C.—Very good, Sir Jonas, that is all I wish to ask you on that especial point.

MR. BOSHLEY.—What was the price

of the shares on the market after the allotment?

SIR JONAS.—The £5 shares, fully paid up, were quoted at £8.

Question.—And what was the last price paid for them?

SIR JONAS.—I believe they are flat on the market, and have been sold for eight shillings each.

MR. BOSHLEY, Q. C.—Then, in general terms, one might say that the pier is flat, the shares are flatter, but the shareholders are flattest of all [loud laughter].

SIR JONAS.—That is entirely a matter of opinion.

Sir Jonas Broadgauge lived at one period of his life in an atmosphere loaded with electricity. Telegrams were flashed to the stock exchange, such as the following:—

"CONSTANTINOPLE, *Thurs.*, 3 P. M.

"Gunboats have arrived from Woolwich. Great excitement prevails. An immediate march on Athens has been discussed. Government 8 per cents. $34\frac{3}{8}$ to $50\frac{3}{4}$; 2 per cents lively at 30. Figs—Markets well supplied and firm."

8 P. M. "Great excitement prevails. War declared. 8 per cents. $2\frac{1}{2}$. Figs no where; no price offered."

"PARIS, *midnight*.

"The Government organs here say that war will be averted. The Greeks, however, say they won't stand (chaff) any more. The "Moniteur" admits this."

"CONSTANTINOPLE, *Saturday*.

"War has been averted, and a new policy has been inaugurated. 8 per cents. are quoted 205 to 209. Figs very firm, and good market for same to-day."

We leave the reader to judge who made money by these rapidly changing accounts of threatened war, and the corresponding difference in prices. We mention no names, we leave it to the reader to surmise; certain it is that there was a way of making money by means of these telegrams—*opes irritamenta malorum*—if availed of properly and by the initiated. We might say of the telegram, as has been said of a certain personage, that it was a liar from the beginning.

Before I conclude, I must not omit to say, that portraits of Sir Jonas Broadgauge, M. P., director of the North and South Junction Railway, may be frequently seen suspended from the walls of the Royal Academy. In some of these portraits he is represented sitting down, and in some he is standing up. Generally the great man is depicted sitting in an easy chair covered with scarlet morocco. Sir Jonas has one hand grasping a roll of parchment, supposed to represent an official document; behind the great man is suspended a map of the Great North and South Junction Railway; and, as the papers state, the face wears an easy and natural expression.

CHAPTER V.

THE SERVANTS IN CHELTENHAM; THE SERVANTS' CLUB; MR. CHARLES HAWKES' SPEECH; MR. SNAFFLES' INTRODUCTION TO THE SERVANTS' CLUB; A SERVANT GIVES UP HIS "APPOINTMENT" BECAUSE THE FAMILY GOES TO HIELAND, THE CLIMATE OF WHICH COUNTRY IS TOO MOIST FOR HIS CONSTITUTION, AND HE WOULD, MOREOVER, GET OUT OF HIS CIRCLE OF ACQUAINTANCE; THE YOUNG SERVANT IN WHITE LIVERY—HIS INEBRIATED CONDITION; HIS RETURN TO HIS MASTER'S HOUSE DESCRIBED; THE AUTHOR'S FAREWELL TO HIS READERS.

The Servants' Club.

Large-calved, broad-shouldered footman *despondingly* to lady of house—

"I miss my carriage exercise."

HAVING already depicted some characters in the upper crust of society in Cheltenham, I will now, with the reader's permission, proceed to describe a few of the characters frequenting the servants' club, situated in High-street, in the above-mentioned town.

About a fortnight after Mrs. Montague Jones' party, a circular came round to a number of the gentlemen (as they call themselves) belonging to this club, intimating that, on Monday, the 1st of March, there would be a ballot for new members, subscriptions for the past year to be paid in, and that there would be a supper afterwards. One of these circulars was placed in the hands of Mr. Brush, Major Golumpus' groom, and he was invited to attend, as he had been, it said, elected a member. Mr. Brush was not a man likely to put his candle under a bushel, and, therefore, proceeded to the club, in company with Charles Hawkes, Mrs. Montague Jones' man, who was most influential, as he was usually voted to the chair for dinner, and was also on the managing committee of the club. "You'll see some very handsome men, and very handsome uniforms," said Mr. Hawkes. "They are a very gentlemanly set of fellows," said Mr. Hawkes, pulling up his shirt collar, "but they chaff a newcomer a bit, just to see what kind of stuff he is made of. They are a good bit stuck up, especially these 'London Bobs,' as we call the London footmen.

We have some capital singers," he continued. "Thomas Green is there to-night, we'll get him to sing 'Champagne Charley,' and 'Hot Taters,' a comic song. Have a cigar?" said Charles Hawkes, as they strolled down the high street, towards the appointed rendezvous; "the governor left a lot of them about," said Hawkes, "and I thought it right to try a dozen of them to see if they agree with me."

They had now arrived at the Plough Hotel, and immediately opposite to this, the reader may remember, a narrow passage runs off the main street; up this they then proceeded, and stopped at the door of a small shop, over which the name *C. Price*, green-grocer, was written.

In Mr. Price's shop window were displayed some cauliflowers, radishes, greens, and also something attractive to the juveniles, in the shape of lollypops, brandy balls, hardbake. There was a notice to this effect—Dinners and Evening Parties attended.

The greengrocer, on the evening above-mentioned, had laid out a long table sufficient to accommodate some sixteen guests; the table linen was tolerably clean, and there were tumblers, and wine-glasses, of various sizes and descriptions, served for each guest. Some of these looked like stout Dutchmen, others like dandies, with taper waists. At each end of the table there was a knife and fork laid for the President and Vice-President. Spittoons, looking something like molehills on the flat surface of the floor, were distributed about here and there. At 8 o'clock the guests began to arrive, and others arriving shortly afterwards, the room became rapidly filled. Some in the glories of plush tights; others in the white cravat and black coat of the butler; here and there a sprinkling of tight-trousered men told that they were of the Snaffles breed, and that they followed equine pursuits. Hawkes introduced Brush as "my partic'lar friend,

Chawles Brush," adding, *sotto voce*, " has travelled a great deal in Hinja."

After the various accounts for the past year had been examined, the committee were chosen for the ensuing year, and Mr. Hawkes, and Snaffles, the Honourable Lionel's groom, were voted President and Vice for the ensuing year. It was then voted by universal consent, *nem. con.* that the supper should be brought up ; and here poor Price's troubles began. A violent pull at the bell brought Price up stairs, who said that the leg of mutton and trimmings would at once be put upon the table ; but instead of this, the gentlemen of the club were kept waiting three minutes, which brought a considerable amount of wrath upon Mr. Price's head, who in truth bore the abuse poured out on him with great meekness.

The covers, or rather the *kivers*, having been removed, Mr. Price was next abused for not attending on sixteen individuals with sufficient alacrity, and being ordered by the President to stand more behind his chair, Price's somewhat soiled hands next attracted the quick eye of Mr. Hawkes.

"How can you have the imprence to wait here without having a washed your 'ands?" said the President. "You are getting woss and woss, Price. Go and show your 'ands to the Vice." Whereupon poor Price had to proceed to the other end of the table to show his hands, but he here commenced an excuse to the general company somewhat thus:—

"Beg pardon, gentlemen—hope you'll excuse me" (cries of "No, we won't"), "but I have been a packing of furniture all day, and it is very hard to keep one's hands clean; I do assure you, gentlemen, that I washed them." "Then, you should use more soap," a gentleman observed. Another—"We don't believe you." Price proceeded—"I am very much obliged, gentlemen, for your patronage, and I will always do my endeavours to please. I have a large family to support, and I hope you won't be hard on me." (Cries of "We won't excuse you.")

"You are an impudent reskel," said a gentleman in green. "You are a hill-bred fellow," said a gentleman in brown. "You are a dissipated fellow," said a gentlemen in grey. "You don't know how to demean yourself," said a gentleman in blue; and thus all the colours and those not in colours hurled their anathemas at Price's devoted head, one gentleman ending, "I would not have him in my house not at *no Price*," the last being the wag of the party. Here there was a loud laugh, and cries of "A pun, a pun." "He is no *prize*," said the same punster; "this is the individual who gives out that he is heir to the Crown, and can prove it by written documents."

Reader, how do you think he does this, why, by showing a letter lately received from his father, who is in the public line, and owns the Crown Hotel, in which he states, that if his son conducts himself properly, and to the writer's satisfaction, that he, the writer, will leave him, at deponent's death, the good-will, fixtures, and furniture, of the Crown Hotel.

The supper having been now brought to a conclusion, there were loud calls for brandy and hot water, and the conversation began to flow still more freely. Some complained of the small pay they received for their services; the old servants hinted the young ones were not up to the same mark as they used to be when they were young, and a good deal of talk was carried on about their masters and mistresses.

Suddenly a young man enters the room, with a somewhat flushed countenance, and a slight appearance of being unsteady in his gait. This individual wore a very elaborate white coat and waistcoat, both of them ornamented with braid, his hair was in powder, and he showed a considerable amount of white stocking.

This was handsome James, Mr. and Mrs. Goldplus' man.

"You really must excuse me, but the champagne was so good, I b'leve I have taken a little too much. I could not resist. Well, I musn't exceed again for some time," said handsome Jeames.

Indeed, the lines of an eminent novelist might be well applied to our white-coated hero.

"A tighter lad, it is confest,
   Ne'er valked with powder in his 'air,
Or vore a nosegay in his breast,
   Than Andsum Jeames of Suffolk-square.

"O evans! it vas the best of sights,
   Behind his master's coach and pair,
To see our Jeames in red-plush tights,
   A driving hoff from Suffolk-square.

"He vel became his hagwillets,
 He cocked his 'at with such a hair,
 His calves and viskers vas such pets,
 That hall loved Jeames of Suffolk-square."

But there is mostly a wish to leave servitude.

"To take a public is my plan,
 And leave this ojus Suffolk-square."

A gentleman in blue then got on his legs and proposed the worthy Presidents. "Anythink he would say in praise of Mr. Hawkes would be superflus, but he couldn't 'elp remindin' them of this, that Mr. Hawkes 'ad been eight years their President, and he was sure hevery one would hadmit that Mr. Hawkes 'ad done more than hany one in

Cheltenham to uphold the Club, and its hexclusiveness and respectability." [Cries of Hear, hear.]

Mr. Hawkes, on rising, was greeted with loud cheers; he said:—" Gentlemen, I thank you very much for the honor you have done me in drinking my health. I must admit that this is one of the proudest moments of my life." [Here Mr. Hawkes took a gulp of brandy and water to help to furbish up some ideas.] " He hoped the Club would go on and prosper; he had done everything in his power to promote the advancement of the Club, and to promote a gentlemanlike feeling amongst them. As to Price, he must admit that he did not give entire satisfaction; he had not a doubt on his mind that the man drank; in fact he appeared to him (Mr. Hawkes) somewhat intoxicated, when he was attending at dinner. From Mr. Hawkes' observations, he came to the conclusion that Price would drink any spirituous liquors he could lay his hands on.

"He intended to speak to him to-morrow, on the subject, and point out to him what a vice intemperance was, and how strongly he would advise him to relinquish such bad habits."

[It may be as well to remark here that the worthy President, having already mixed his ninth tumbler, would appear to be peculiarly adapted to speak on the subject of intemperance to Price.] The President concluded by remarking that at the solicitation of some Members they had started a Derby sweep, [and here he was interrupted by a slight hiccup], and it would be expected of the winner [hiccup repeated] to give them a dinner.

Mr. Hawkes again rose to add a few remarks. By the original rules of the Club only gentlemen's footmen could become Members; he now begged to state that not only grooms and valets, but that coachmen were admitted to the advantages of the Club.

A gentleman here arose; he wished

to make a few remarks; he had resigned his present situation; the family were going to Hireland, and as he heard the climate was damp and hard to get good hale there, and as he also considered he would get out of his *circle of acquaintance*, and would not also enjoy the sociability and good fellowship of the Club, there was no alternative open to him but to *resign :* besides, he had an objection to the place for a considerable time, as he considered the colour of his uniform did not altogether suit his complexion; if any of his hearers could help him to procure a place, he would not forget them.

Another said he had resigned also. He had asked lately for an increased remuneration; the govenor answered, " Why, do you know that you are better off than Ensigns in the Line?" "Really, now, Sir, I answered, I don't think it is fair for to go to compare me to an Ensign, when I am so superior in domestic accomplishments to the greater part of them." [Cries of Bravo! Jenkins, from the gentlemen of the Club.]

The evening entertainment was now drawing to a close; as it was half past eleven o'clock most of the Members had left, but Brush, who had his eye on the handsome footman, and wished to take down some of his bounce, as he termed it, kept encouraging him on in the consumption of brandy and water, till having accomplished his purpose of making him worship deeply at the shrine of Bacchus, volunteered to see him safe home to Suffolk-square; but previously to escorting him home, and rousing him out of a drowsy fit he had fallen into, he corked his face black with a burnt cork, then turned his white coat inside out, and chalking D. and I. for drunk and incapable, on the back of the coat, rang the area bell, then propped him against the door, and leaving him, proceeded homewards with a light step, and whistling a jaunty air.

Reader, my observations on Cheltenham life and character have now come to a close. I hope that, should you go to Cheltenham, you may experience as kind a reception and as much genuine hospitality as the writer has experienced at the house of Mrs. Montague Jones; and if you do not go to Mrs. Jones' house, certainly at others in the town you will meet Captain Hee Haw, M. C. The Honorable Lionel will also be seen as long certainly as the cash lasts, which I hope will, for a very long time. Mr. Jelly, I have no doubt, will be found also, unless he has migrated to some other watering place, on a temporary excursion. The young ladies I am not so sure about, I mean the identical

The Servants' Club.

ladies described. Miss Deuxtemps may have called in the services of the Rev. Mr. Dovecote and got married at that pretty country church outside Cheltenham, with the long avenue of trees up to the porch, as *people are so stared at in the Parish church*. It will be Miss F. Smiles' own fault if she retains her present name long; but Mrs. Whitmore will, I presume, be there still, and still the *on dit* will be that another novel is forthcoming, even better than the last. The last individual I shall notice is the gallant Major. I think that, during each revolving winter, you will see the Major at his old haunts, and that he will still continue to tell his wonderful stories and give as good champagne, moselle, claret and port as ever; and if I am not much mistaken a dinner invitation to the Major's house will be still much sought after.

Before I conclude, I beg to thank my many kind friends in Cheltenham for the hospitality evinced towards the writer; and having said this much, I beg to make my best bow to the reader, and hope that perchance we may yet meet again.

THE END.

Clarendon House, upon the site and with the materials of which 74, Piccadilly, was built.—See EVELYN *and* PEPYS.

VERY IMPORTANT NEW BOOKS.
Special List for 1872.

⁂ NOTE.—In order to ensure the correct delivery of the actual Works or Particular Editions specified in this List, the Name of the Publisher SHOULD BE DISTINCTLY GIVEN. *Stamps or a Post-Office Order may be remitted direct to the Publisher, who will forward per return.*

*When "*DIRECT APPLICATION*" is requested, the Trade will please communicate with Mr. Hotten.*

A Splendid New Gift-Book.

The uncertain and evanescent character of all books illustrated by Photography is so well known, that it was thought a Gathering of our finest Modern Paintings, engraved upon Steel in the highest style of art, would form an acceptable Gift-Book.

BEAUTIFUL PICTURES BY BRITISH ARTISTS.

A Gathering of Favourites from our Picture Galleries, 1800–1870. Including examples by WILKIE, CONSTABLE, J. M. W. TURNER, MULREADY, Sir EDWIN LANDSEER, MACLISE, LESLIE, E. M. WARD, FRITH, JOHN GILBERT, ANSDELL, MARCUS STONE, Sir NOEL PATON, EYRE CROWE, O'NEIL, FAED, MADOX BROWN. All Engraved in the highest style of Art by the most Eminent English Engravers. Edited, with Notices of the Artists, by SYDNEY ARMYTAGE, M.A. The whole forming a Magnificent Volume, in imperial 4to, bound in Byzantine cloth gilt, 21*s.*

⁂ *The value of the Paintings here indelibly reflected by the engraver's art is estimated at* £50,000. IT IS AN ART BOOK FOR ALL TIME.

AARON PENLEY'S SKETCHING IN WATER COLOURS. 21*s.*

By the Author of "The English School of Painting in Water-Colours," &c. ILLUSTRATED WITH BEAUTIFUL CHROMO-LITHOGRAPHS, produced with the utmost care to resemble original WATER-COLOUR DRAWINGS. Small folio, the text tastefully printed, in handsome binding, gilt edges, suitable for the Drawing-room table, price 21*s.*

⁂ *It has long been felt that the magnificent work of the great English master of Painting in Water-colours, published at £4 4s., was too dear for general circulation. The above embodies all the instructions of the distinguished author, with fine Specimens of Water-colour Painting.* A MOST CHARMING PRESENT FOR A YOUNG LADY.

JOHN CAMDEN HOTTEN, 74 AND 75, PICCADILLY, LONDON.

Very Important New Books.

A truly Magnificent Work.
"LIVES OF THE SAINTS." Enriched with 51 exquisite Full-page Miniatures, in Gold and Colours. Every page of the Text within Engraved Borders of Beautiful Design. In thick 4to, sumptuously printed, and bound in silk velvet, enriched with gold, preserved in a case, £7 7s.; in morocco, extra gilt, inlaid, £10 15s.

THIS VERY IMPORTANT WORK, commenced three years since, has at length been completed, and fully justifies the high expectations formed of it during its progress through the press. Taking the text of the Rev. Alban Butler as his guide, the Editor has, wherever practicable, carefully verified the references of that eminent divine. The delicacy and finish of the beautiful miniatures have never before been approached in any similar work in this country. They exhibit a beauty and exquisite softness of colour which have hitherto only been realized by the most expensive miniature paintings. The work must be seen to be appreciated, as it is like no other of the kind. The preparation has been so costly and slow, that the book is never likely to decrease in value.

A very Splendid Volume.
SAINT URSULA, Princess of Britain, and her Companions. With 25 Full-Page 4to Illuminated Miniatures from the Pictures of Cologne, and exquisitely designed Woodcut Borders. In crown 4to, beautifully bound in satin and gold, £3 15s.

*** THE FINEST BOOK-PAINTINGS OF THE KIND EVER PUBLISHED. THE ARTIST OBTAINED THE GOLD PRIZE AT THE PARIS EXPOSITION.

THE BOOK MUST BE SEEN TO BE APPRECIATED. The Illustrations are exact reproductions of the exquisite paintings of the Van Eyck school, and in finish and beauty are far above any similar book-paintings issued in this country. As the preparation of the work has been so costly and slow, it is never likely to decrease in value.

Exquisite Miniatures and Illuminations.
"GOLDEN VERSES FROM THE NEW TESTAMENT." With 50 Illuminations and Miniatures from celebrated Missals and Books of Hours of the 14th and 15th Centuries, in Gold and Colours. The Text very beautifully printed in Letters of Gold on fine Ivory Paper. 4to, in a handsome cloth case, with silk ribbons, 30s.; or bound in a volume, morocco, gilt edges, £2 5s.

ALBERT DURER'S "LITTLE PASSION," as Engraved by the distinguished Artist in 1509-10; consisting of 37 inimitable Designs upon Wood. With a Survey of Durer's Works by W. C. PRIME. Royal 4to. The Illustrations in exquisite facsimile, emblematic binding, 25s.

*** *Only 100 copies of this beautiful book were printed.*

BRUNET'S MANUEL DU LIBRAIRE, 5 vols. royal 8vo, half morocco, top edge gilt, 25s. only.

JOHN CAMDEN HOTTEN, 74 AND 75, PICCADILLY, LONDON.

Very Important New Books.

CURIOSITIES OF LONDON. Exhibiting the most Rare and Remarkable Objects of Interest in the Metropolis; with nearly Sixty Years' Personal Recollections. By JOHN TIMBS, F.S.A. New Edition, Corrected and Enlarged, 21s.

⁎ "*A most valuable and interesting work, and a mine of information to all who desire any particulars about London, past and present. It contains nearly 1,000 closely printed pages.*"

Bow Church and Cheapside, 1750.

LONDON CHARACTERS: *The Humour, Pathos, and Peculiarities of London Life.* By HENRY MAYHEW (Author of "London Labour and the London Poor") and other Writers. With upwards of 70 Characteristic Illustrations of London Life. Crown 8vo, 480 pages, 7s. 6d.

KNIGHT'S (Charles) PICTORIAL HISTORY OF LONDON, *Ancient and Modern.* With nearly 700 Engravings of Buildings, Antiquities, Costumes, Remarkable Characters, Curiosities, &c., &c. 6 vols., imp. 8vo, bound in 3, cloth neat, 35s.

⁎ *The most delightful book ever written about Old and Modern London. It is a perfect mine of information, and should be in every English Library. If looked at from the point of cheapness alone, the work is a perfect marvel, containing as it does more than 2,500 large and handsomely printed pages, crowded with pictures.*

JOHN CAMDEN HOTTEN, 74 AND 75, PICCADILLY, LONDON.

Very Important New Books.

THE HISTORY OF ADVERTISING, in all Ages and Countries. A Companion to the "HISTORY OF SIGNBOARDS." With many very amusing Anecdotes and Examples of Successful Advertisers. By Messrs. LARWOOD and HOTTEN. [*In preparation.*

MARY HOLLIS : A Romance of the Days of Charles I. and William Prince of Orange. From the Dutch of H. J. SCHIMMEL, "the Sir Walter Scott of Holland." 3 vols., cr. 8vo, £1 11s. 6d.

*** *This novel relates to one of the most interesting periods of our history. It has created the greatest excitement on the Continent, where it quickly passed through several editions. It is now translated from the Dutch with the assistance of the author.*

New Series of Illustrated Humorous Novels.

1. THE STORY OF A HONEYMOON. By CHAS. H. ROSS and AMBROSE CLARKE. With numerous Illustrations, crown 8vo, cloth gilt, 6s.

*** *An inimitable story of the adventures and troubles of a newly-married couple. Not unlike Mr. Burnand's "Happy Thoughts."*

2. CENT. PER CENT. : A Story Written upon a Bill Stamp. By BLANCHARD JERROLD. With numerous Illustrations. Crown 8vo, cloth gilt, 6s.

*** *A capital novel, "intended not only for City readers, but for all interested in money matters."*—*Athenæum.*

MELCHIOR GORLES. By HENRY AITCHENBIE. 3 vols., 8vo, £1 11s. 6d.

*** *The New Novel, illustrative of "Mesmeric Influence," or whatever else we may choose to term that strange power which some persons exercise over others.*

YANKEE DROLLERIES. Edited by GEORGE AUGUSTUS SALA. Containing ARTEMUS WARD, BIGLOW PAPERS, ORPHEUS C. KERR, MAJOR JACK DOWNING, and NASBY PAPERS. One of the Cheapest Books ever published. New Edition, on toned paper, cloth extra, 700 pages, 3s. 6d.

MORE YANKEE DROLLERIES. A Second Series of Celebrated Works by the best American Humorists. ARTEMUS WARD'S TRAVELS ; HANS BREITMANN ; PROFESSOR AT THE BREAKFAST-TABLE ; BIGLOW PAPERS, Part II. ; JOSH BILLINGS. Introduction by G. A. SALA. Cr. 8vo, 700 pages, cloth extra, 3s. 6d.

Third Supply of YANKEE DROLLERIES. The best recent Works of American Humorists. A. WARD'S FENIANS, MARK TWAIN, AUTOCRAT OF THE BREAKFAST TABLE, BRET HARTE, INNOCENTS ABROAD. Introduction by G. A. SALA. Crown 8vo, 700 pages, cloth extra, 3s. 6d.

*** *An entirely new gathering of Transatlantic humour. Fourteen thousand copies have been sold of the first and second series.*

JOHN CAMDEN HOTTEN, 74 AND 75, PICCADILLY, LONDON.

Very Important New Books.

GEORGE COLMAN'S HUMOROUS WORKS.

BROAD GRINS. My Nightgown and *Slippers*, and other Humorous Works, Prose and Poetical, of GEORGE COLMAN the Younger. Now first collected, with Life and Anecdotes of the Author, by GEORGE B. BUCKSTONE. Crown 8vo, 500 pages, 7s. 6d.

*** *Admirers of genuine old English wit and humour—irresistible and always fresh—will be delighted with the collected edition of George Colman's humorous works. As a wit, he has had no equal in our time; and a man with a tithe of his ability could, at the present day, make the fortune of any one of our so-called "comic journals," and bankrupt the rest.*

Are you Engaged? If so, procure
ADVICE TO PARTIES ABOUT TO MARRY. A Series of Instructions in Jest and Earnest. By the Hon. HUGH ROWLEY. With Humorous Illustrations. Price 3s. 6d., elegantly bound.

*** *Before taking the "awful plunge" be sure to consult this little work. If it is not a guarantee against life-long misery, it will at least be found of great assistance in selecting a partner for life.*

SEYMOUR'S SKETCHES. A Companion Volume to "Leech's Pictures." The Book of Cockney Sports, Whims, and Oddities. Nearly 200 highly amusing Illustrations. Oblong 4to, a handsome volume, half morocco, price 12s.

*** *A re-issue of the famous pictorial comicalities which were so popular thirty years ago. The volume is admirably adapted for a table-book, and the pictures will doubtless again meet with that popularity which was extended towards them when the artist projected with Mr. Dickens the famous "Pickwick Papers."*

THE GENIAL SHOWMAN; or, Adventures with Artemus Ward, and the Story of his Life. By E. P. HINGSTON, companion of Artemus Ward during the latter's Adventures. Cheap and popular Edition, cr. 8vo, illustrated by Brunton, 7s. 6d.

*** *This is a most interesting work. It gives Sketches of Show-Life in the Far West, on the Pacific Coast, among the Mines of California, in Salt Lake City, and across the Rocky Mountains; including chapters descriptive of Artemus Ward's visit to England.*

JOHN CAMDEN HOTTEN, 74 AND 75, PICCADILLY, LONDON.

Very Important New Books.

Capital Shilling Books.

BISMARCK: The Story of his Career, told for Popular Reading. By Mr. GEO. BULLEN, of the British Museum. 1s.

⁎⁎⁎ An admirable account of the "Man of Blood and Iron;" giving numerous very characteristic anecdotes.

THE CONSCRIPT: A Story of the French and German War of 1813. By MM. ERCKMANN-CHATRIAN. 1s.

⁎⁎⁎ The only unabridged English translation published.

WATERLOO. A Story of the War of 1814. By MM. ERCKMANN-CHATRIAN. The only unabridged translation. 1s.

KILLED AT SAARBRÜCK: An Englishman's Adventures during the War. By EDWARD LEGGE, Correspondent at the Seat of War. Cloth, 2s. 6d.; paper, 1s.

NEVER CAUGHT: The thrilling Narrative of a Blockade Runner during the American War. 1s.

CHIPS FROM A ROUGH LOG. Amusing Account of a Voyage to the Antipodes. 1s.

THACKERAY, the Humourist and Man of Letters. A Story of his Life. By the Author of the "Life of Dickens." 1s.

HOWARD PAUL'S New Story Book, Lord BYRON in LOVE, &c. 1s.

MYSTERY OF MR. E. DROOD. A delightful Adaptation. By ORPHEUS C. KERR. 1s.

POLICEMAN Y: His Opinions on War and the Millingtary. With Illustrations by SODEN. Cloth, 2s. 6d.; paper, 1s.

⁎⁎⁎ Readers of "Thackeray's "Policeman X Ballads" will be much amused with the "Opinions" of his brother officer, "Policeman Y."

BIGLOW PAPERS. By J. R. LOWELL. The best and fullest edition of these Humorous and very Clever Verses. 1s.

ORPHEUS C. KERR [Office-Seeker] PAPERS. By R. S. NEWELL. A most mirth-provoking work. 1s.

JOSH BILLINGS: His Book of Sayings. Exceedingly droll, and of world-wide reputation. 1s.

VERE VEREKER'S VENGEANCE. By TOM HOOD. A delightful piece of humour. Idiotically illustrated by BRUNTON. 1s.

WIT AND HUMOUR. Verses by O. W. HOLMES, Author of the "Autocrat of the Breakfast Table." 1s.

JOHN CAMDEN HOTTEN, 74 AND 75, PICCADILLY, LONDON.

Very Important New Books.

THE STANDARD EDITION.

ROBINSON CRUSOE. Profusely Illustrated by ERNEST GRISET. Edited, with a New Account of the Origin of Robinson Crusoe, by WILLIAM LEE, Esq. Crown 8vo, 5s.

** *This edition deserves special attention from the fact that it is the only correct one that has been printed since the time of Defoe. By the kindness of Mr. Lee a copy of the rare and valuable original, in three vols., was deposited with the printers during the progress of the work, and all those alterations and blunders which have been discovered in every recent edition are in this case avoided. There is no living artist better adapted to the task of illustrating Crusoe than Ernest Griset.*

LEGENDS OF SAVAGE LIFE. By JAMES GREENWOOD, the famous Author of "A Night in a Workhouse." With 36 inimitably droll Illustrations, drawn and coloured by ERNEST GRISET, the English Gustave Doré. 4to, coloured, 7s. 6d.; plain, 5s.

** *The pictures are among the most surprising which have come from this artist's pencil.*

"A Munchausen sort of book. The drawings by M. Griset are very powerful and eccentric."—*Saturday Review.*

Walk up! Walk up! and see the

FOOL'S PARADISE; with the Many Wonderful Adventures there, as seen in the strange, surprising

PEEP-SHOW OF PROFESSOR WOLLEY COBBLE,
Raree Showman these Five-and-Twenty Years.

N.B.—Money Returned if the Performance not Approved of. Private Parties attended on the Shortest Notice. Price 7s. 6d.

Crown 4to, with nearly 200 immensely funny Pictures, all beautifully Coloured.

THE PROFESSOR'S LEETLE MUSIC LESSON.
** *One of the drollest, most comical books ever published.*

THE HATCHET-THROWERS. With Thirty-six Illustrations, coloured after the inimitably grotesque Drawings of ERNEST GRISET. 4to, cloth gilt, 7s. 6d.; plates uncoloured, 5s.

** *Comprises the astonishing adventures of Three Ancient Mariners, the Brothers Brass of Bristol, Mr. Corker, and Mungo Midge.*

JOHN CAMDEN HOTTEN, 74 AND 75, PICCADILLY, LONDON.

Very Important New Books.

WORKS BY BRET HARTE.
WIDELY KNOWN FOR THEIR EXQUISITE PATHOS AND DELIGHTFUL HUMOUR.

☞ BLACKWOOD'S MAGAZINE *goes into raptures over this Author, and gives page after page to prove that he is a literary star of undoubted brilliancy.*

1. **LUCK OF ROARING CAMP, and other Stories.** By BRET HARTE. Crown 8vo, toned paper, 3s. 6d.; a paper edition, 1s.
*** *The* "Saturday Review" *devoted three columns to the praise of these marvellous stories.* "Chambers's Journal" *gives several pages under the heading,* "A New Transatlantic Genius." *The* "Spectator" *is delighted with this new author; and readers are everywhere asking for his books.*

2. **THAT HEATHEN CHINEE, and other Humorous Poems.** By BRET HARTE. Cloth, very neat, 2s. 6d.; paper, 1s. 6d.
*** *An entirely new style of humour. Since the publication of these poems in this country, extracts from them have been copied and re-copied into every newspaper throughout the country, giving the public an infinity of delight.*

3. **SENSATION NOVELS.** Condensed by BRET HARTE. Price 2s. 6d., cloth, neat; or, in paper, 1s. 6d.
*** *A most enjoyable book. Here are the titles of some of the* "Sensation Novels:" SELINA SEDILIA: by Miss M. E. B-dd-n and Mrs. H-n-y W-d. FANTINE: after the French of Victor Hugo. TERENCE DEUVILLE: by Ch-l-s L-v-r. THE DWELLER ON THE THRESHOLD: by Sir Ed-d L-tt-n B-lw-r. THE NINETY-NINE GUARDSMEN: by Al-x-a-d-r D-m-s. MR. MIDSHIPMAN BREEZY, A Naval Officer: by Captain M-rry-t, R.N. GUY HEAVYSTONE; or, "ENTIRE:" A Muscular Novel: by the Author of "Sword and Gun." THE HAUNTED MAN: A Christmas Story: by Ch-r-s D-c-k-ns. MARY MCGILLUP: A Southern Novel: after Belle Boyd. MISS MIX: by Ch-l-tte Br-ntë. NO TITLE: by W-lk-e C-ll-ns.

4. **LOTHAW: or, The Adventures of a Young Gentleman** *in Search of a Religion.* By Mr. BENJAMINS *(Bret Harte).* Price 6d. Curiously Illustrated.
*** *A most mirth-making little volume. Readers of a recent popular novel will enjoy it with considerable relish. It is so droll, so entirely new, that it cannot fail to amuse.*

5. **Illustrated Edition of THAT HEATHEN CHINEE, and** *Poems.* By BRET HARTE. With "That Heathen Chinee" set to Music by STEPHEN TUCKER, Author of "Beautiful Isle of the Sea." Cloth, very neat, 3s. 6d.
*** *These are the Illustrations which have so tickled our American cousins. There's a sort of "kick-up-your-heels" delight about them. In a word, they're* immense!

6. **EAST AND WEST.** The *New* Volume of Verse. By BRET HARTE, Author of "That Heathen Chinee." Cloth, very neat, 2s. 6d.; or in paper, 1s. 6d.
*** *Readers who found pleasure in reading this Author's first books will not be disappointed with this new work.*

COMPANION TO BRET HARTE'S "HEATHEN CHINEE."

LITTLE BREECHES, and other Pieces, Descriptive and *Pathetic.* By Col. JOHN HAY. Cloth, neat, 2s. 6d.; in paper, 1s. 6d.
*** *The dramatic fire and vigour of these PIKE COUNTY BALLADS will startle English readers. The last lines of the first ballad are simply terrific,—something entirely different from what any English author would dream of, much less put on paper.*

JOHN CAMDEN HOTTEN, 74 AND 75, PICCADILLY, LONDON.

Very Important New Books.

NEW BOOK ON THE LONDON PARKS.

THE STORY OF THE LONDON PARKS. By JACOB LARWOOD.
With *numerous Illustrations*, COLOURED AND PLAIN. Vol. I., Hyde Park; Vol. II., St. James's Park and the Green Park. Price 18s. the Two Volumes.

*** *This is a new and most interesting work, giving a complete History of these favourite out-of-door resorts, from the earliest period to the present time. The fashions, the promenades, the rides, the reviews, and other displays in the Parks, from the merry days of Charles II. down to the present airings in Rotten Row and drives "around the ring," are all fully given, together with the exploits of bold highwaymen and the duels of rival lovers, and other appellants to the Code of Honour.*

SKETCHES OF IRISH CHARACTER. By Mrs. S. C. HALL.
With numerous Illustrations on Steel and Wood, by DANIEL MACLISE, R.A., JOHN GILBERT, W. HARVEY, and G. CRUIKSHANK. 8vo, pp. 450, cloth, gilt edges, 7s. 6d.

*** *One of the most delightful of this favourite Author's works. As a picture of Irish domestic life it has no superior.*

"The Irish Sketches of this lady resemble Miss Mitford's beautiful English Sketches in 'Our Village,' but they are far more vigorous and picturesque and bright."—*Blackwood's Magazine.*

DROLLS OF OLD CORNWALL; or, Popular Romances of
the West of England. Collected and Edited by ROBERT HUNT, F.R.S. New Popular Edition, complete in one vol., with Illustrations by GEORGE CRUIKSHANK. Price 7s. 6d.

*** "Mr. Hunt's charming book on the Drolls and Stories of the West of England."—*Saturday Review.*

JOHN CAMDEN HOTTEN, 74 AND 75, PICCADILLY, LONDON.

Very Important New Books.

WORKS BY MARK TWAIN.
WIDELY KNOWN FOR THEIR FRESH AND DELIGHTFUL HUMOUR.

1.—*PLEASURE TRIP ON THE CONTINENT OF EUROPE.*
By MARK TWAIN. 500 pages, 2s.; or in cloth, 3s.

*** TWAIN'S PLEASURE TRIP *is also issued in two-vol. form under the title of*

2.—*"THE INNOCENTS ABROAD."* By MARK TWAIN.
THE VOYAGE OUT. Cloth, neat, fine toned paper, "SUPERIOR EDITION," 3s. 6d.; or in paper, 1s.

3.—*THE NEW PILGRIM'S PROGRESS.* By MARK TWAIN.
THE VOYAGE HOME. Cloth, neat, fine toned paper, "SUPERIOR EDITION," 3s. 6d.; or in paper, 1s.

*** *Readers who approved of this Author's quaint story of "The Jumping Frog," will be very well satisfied with the "New Pilgrim's Progress:" there has been no work like it issued here for years.*

4.—*BURLESQUE "AUTOBIOGRAPHY," "FIRST MEDIÆVAL ROMANCE," AND "ON CHILDREN."* By MARK TWAIN. 6d.

5.—*THE JUMPING FROG, and other Humorous Sketches.*
By MARK TWAIN. 1s.
"An inimitably funny book."—*Saturday Review.*

6.— *EYE-OPENERS.* A volume of immensely Funny Sayings, and Stories that will bring a smile upon the gruffest countenance. By the celebrated MARK TWAIN. Cloth, neat, 2s. 6d.; Cheap Paper Edition, 1s.

7.—*SCREAMERS.* A Gathering of Delicious Bits and Short Stories, by the renowned MARK TWAIN. Cloth, neat, 5s. 6d.; Cheap Paper Edition, 1s.

JOHN CAMDEN HOTTEN, 74 AND 75, PICCADILLY LONDON.

Very Important New Books.

MAGICIAN'S OWN BOOK. Containing Ample Instructions for PERFORMANCE in LEGERDEMAIN, CUPS and BALLS, EGGS, HATS, HANDKERCHIEFS, &c. By the Author of "The Secret Out." All from Actual Experience, and Edited by W. H. CREMER, Jun., of Regent Street. With 200 Illustrations, 4s. 6d.

THE SECRET OUT; or, One Thousand Tricks with Cards, and other Recreations; with Entertaining Experiments in Drawing-Room or "White Magic." By the Author of the "Magician's Own Book." Edited by W. H. CREMER, Jun., of Regent Street. With 300 Engravings. Crown 8vo, cloth, 4s. 6d.

*** *These Books are complete Cyclopædias of Legerdemain. Under the title of "Le Magicien des Salons" the first has long been a standard Magic Book with all French and German Professors of the Art. The tricks are described so carefully, with engravings to illustrate them, that anybody can easily learn how to perform them.*

ENTIRELY NEW GAMES.

THE MERRY CIRCLE. A Book of NEW, GRACEFUL, and INTELLECTUAL GAMES and AMUSEMENTS. Edited by Mrs. CLARA BELLEW. Crown 8vo, numerous Illustrations, 4s. 6d.

*** *A new and capital book of Household Amusements. These are in every way Intellectual Games, and will please both old and young. It is an excellent book to consult before going to an evening party.*

THE ART OF AMUSING. A Collection of Graceful Arts, Games, Tricks, Puzzles, and Charades, intended to amuse everybody, and enable all to amuse everybody else. By FRANK BELLEW With nearly 300 Illustrations. Crown 8vo, 4s. 6d.

*** *One of the most entertaining handbooks for amusement ever published.*

NOTICE.—*Of the four books offered above, the first is the most Advanced in the Mysteries of White Magic. The second is a capital Beginners' Book on the Wonderful Art of Conjuring. The third work, "The Merry Circle," is a book of an Advanced Character in Family Amusements, and requires considerable judgment on the part of the players. The last work is a capital introductory book to the Art of Amusing generally.*

JOHN CAMDEN HOTTEN, 74 AND 75, PICCADILLY, LONDON.

Very Important New Books.

WORKS OF THE LATE ARTEMUS WARD.

New Edition, price 1s.; by post 1s. 2d.

ARTEMUS WARD: HIS BOOK. The Author's Enlarged Edition. With Notes and Introduction by the Editor of the "Biglow Papers." One of the wittiest, and certainly one of the most mirth-provoking, books published for many years. Containing the whole of the Original, with the following extra chapters:—Babes in the Wood; Tavern Accommodation, Betsy-Jain-Re-Organized; A. Ward's First Umbrella; Brigham Young's Wives; Artemus Ward's Brother; Mormon Bill of Fare.

NOTICE.—*Mr. Hotten's Edition is the only one published in this country with the sanction of the Author.*

The *Saturday Review* says of Mr. Hotten's edition: "The author combines the powers of Thackeray with those of Albert Smith. The salt is rubbed in by a native hand—one which has the gift of tickling."

"We never, not even in the pages of our best humorists, read anything so laughable and so shrewd as we have seen in this book by the mirthful Artemus."—*Public Opinion.*

ARTEMUS WARD: His Travels Among the Mormons
and on the Rampage. Edited by E. P. HINGSTON, the Agent and Companion of A. WARD whilst "on the Rampage." New Edition, price 1s.

*** *Some of Artemus's most mirth-provoking papers are to be found in this book. The chapters upon the Mormons will unbend the sternest countenance. As bits of fun they are* IMMENSE!

ARTEMUS WARD AMONG THE FENIANS: with the *Showman's Experiences of Life at Washington, and Military Ardour at Baldinsville.* Toned paper, price 6d.; by post, 7d.

ARTEMUS WARD'S LECTURE AT THE EGYPTIAN HALL, with the Panorama. Edited by the late T. W. ROBERTSON (Author of "Caste," "Ours," "Society," &c.) and E. P. HINGSTON. Small 4to, exquisitely printed, bound in green and gold, with NUMEROUS TINTED ILLUSTRATIONS, price 6s.

"Mr. Hotten has conceived the happy idea of printing Artemus Ward's 'Lecture' in such a way as to afford the reader an accurate notion of the emphasis, by-play, &c., with which it was delivered. We have no hesitation in saying that Mr. Hotten has almost restored the great humourist to the flesh."—*Daily Telegraph.*

"The tomahawk fell from our hands as we roared with laughter—the pipe of peace slipped from between our lips as our eyes filled with tears! Laughter for Artemus's wit—tears for his untimely death! This book is a record of both. Those who never saw Artemus in the flesh, let them read of him in the spirit."—*Tomahawk.*

"It actually reproduces Ward's Lecture, which was brimful of first-class wit and humour."—*Daily News.*

"It keeps you in fits of laughter."—*Leader.*

"One of the choice and curious volumes for the issue of which Mr. Hotten has become famous." —*City Press.*

"The Lecture is not alone droll: it is full of information."—*Examiner.*

"It adds one to our books of genuine fun."—*Sunday Times.*

12mo, 200 pages, 1s. 6d.; or cloth, neat, 2s.

ARTEMUS WARD IN LONDON. Comprising the Letters to "Punch," and other Humorous Papers, now first collected.

*** *Contains some quaint and humorous compositions which were found upon the author's table after his decease.*

ARTEMUS WARD, Complete. The Works of CHARLES FARRER BROWNE, better known as "ARTEMUS WARD," now first collected. Crown 8vo, with fine Portrait, facsimile of handwriting, &c., 540 pages, cloth neat, 7s. 6d.

*** *Comprises all that the humourist was written in England or America. Admirers of poor Artemus Ward will be glad to possess his writings in a complete form.*

JOHN CAMDEN HOTTEN, 74 AND 75, PICCADILLY, LONDON.

Very Important New Books.

FLAGELLATION and the FLAGELLANTS; A History of the
Rod in all Countries, from the Earliest Period to the Present Time. By the Rev. WILLIAM COOPER, B.A. With numerous Illustrations. Thick crown 8vo, 12s. 6d.

THE ROD	THE BIRCH
IN	IN
THE CHURCH,	THE FAMILY,
CONVENT,	LADIES' SEMINARIES,
MONASTERY,	BOYS' SCHOOLS,
PRISON,	COLLEGES,
ARMY, NAVY,	
IN PUBLIC	THE BOUDOIR,
AND	
IN PRIVATE.	Ancient and Modern.

₊ "A very remarkable, and certainly a very readable volume. Those who care for quaint stories of the birch will find much matter for reflection, and not a little amusement, in Mr. Cooper's 'Flagellation' Book."—*Daily Telegraph.*

The ENGLISHMAN'S HOUSE, from a Cottage to a Mansion.
A Practical Guide to Members of Building Societies, and all interested in Selecting or Building a House. By C. J. RICHARDSON, Architect, Author of "Old English Mansions," &c. Second Edition, Corrected and Enlarged, with nearly 600 Illustrations. Crown 8vo, 550 pages, cloth, 7s. 6d.

₊ This Work might not inappropriately be termed "A Book of Houses." It gives every variety of house, from a workman's cottage to a nobleman's palace. The book is intended to supply a want long felt, viz., a plain non-technical account of every style of house, with the cost and manner of building.

JOHN CAMDEN HOTTEN, 74 AND 75, PICCADILLY, LONDON.

Very Important New Books.

RUSKIN AND CRUIKSHANK. "German Popular Stories." Collected by the Brothers GRIMM. Translated by EDGAR TAYLOR. Edited by JOHN RUSKIN. With Twenty-two Illustrations after the inimitable designs of GEORGE CRUIKSHANK. BOTH SERIES COMPLETE. Cloth, 8vo, 6s. 6d.; gilt leaves, 7s. 6d.

*** *These are the designs which Mr. Ruskin has praised so highly, placing them far above all Cruikshank's other works of a similar character. So rare had the original book (published in 1823–1826) become, that £5 to £6 per copy was an ordinary price.*

"FAMILY FAIRY TALES;" or, Glimpses of Elfland at Heatherston Hall. Edited by CHOLMONDELEY PENNELL, Author of "Puck on Pegasus," &c. Adorned with beautiful Pictures of "My Lord Lion," "King Uggermugger," and other Great Folks. Handsomely printed on toned paper, in cloth, green and gold, price 4s. 6d. plain, 5s. 6d. coloured.

*** *This charming volume has been universally praised by the critical press.*

SCHOOL LIFE AT WINCHESTER COLLEGE; or, The Reminiscences of a Winchester Junior. By the Author of "The Log of the Water Lily," and "The Water Lily on the Danube." Second Edition, Revised, COLOURED PLATES, 7s. 6d.

*** *This book does for Winchester what "Tom Brown's School Days" did for Rugby.*

PRINCE UBBELY BUBBLE'S NEW STORY BOOK. The Dragon all Covered with Spikes; The Long-tailed Nag; The Three One-legged Men; The Old Fly and the Young Fly; Tom and the Ogre; and many other Tales. By J. TEMPLETON LUCAS. With numerous Illustrations by MATT MORGAN, BARNES, GORDON THOMPSON, BRUNTON, and other Artists. In small 4to, green and gold, 4s. 6d.; gilt leaves, 5s. 6d.

*** *The Times devoted a special column in praise of this New Story Book.*

MADGE AND THE FAIRY CONTENT. A charming Child's Story. By BLANCHARD JERROLD. Intended to inculcate a spirit of Contentment. With nearly 100 Pictures of the Industry requisite to produce the Christmas Pudding. 4s. 6d.

LITTLE CHARLIE'S LIFE OF HIMSELF. Edited by the Rev. W. R. CLARK, M.A., Vicar of Taunton. 4to, cloth, full of curious Illustrations, 3s. 6d.

*** *A most amusing Present for a child. It is an exact facsimile of the autobiography of a boy between six and seven years of age, as written by himself in his copy-book.*

JOHN CAMDEN HOTTEN, 74 AND 75, PICCADILLY, LONDON.

Very Important New Books.

GUSTAVE DORÉ'S MOST CHARACTERISTIC WORKS.

RABELAIS. Faithfully translated from the French, with variorum Notes, and numerous characteristic Illustrations by GUSTAVE DORÉ. Cloth neat, 600 pages. Price 7s. 6d.

*** *When it is stated that this is a "faithful translation," scholars will know what is meant. The 60 full-page Illustrations are in the Artist's best and most fantastic manner.*

COCKAYNES IN PARIS, The; or, an English Family Abroad. By BLANCHARD JERROLD. With MOST AMUSING thumb-nail SKETCHES of the ENGLISH by GUSTAVE DORÉ, taken on the Rail, the Steam-boat, and the Pavement. Price 7s. 6d.

*** *Returned tourists who would like to see themselves from a French point of view, will be greatly diverted with this new travel-book. The pictures are very droll, and give the exact notions of foreigners concerning us. One of these notions is that all English ladies and gentlemen breathe through their mouths instead of through their noses, hence our mouths are always open, our teeth protrude, and we are continually on the grin. Some of their caricatures of our weaknesses are not wholly devoid of truth.*

CAPTAIN CASTAGNETTE: His Surprising, almost Incredible Adventures. 4to, with GUSTAVE DORÉ'S Illustrations. Price 1s. 9d. (sells at 5s.)   *Apply DIRECT to Mr. HOTTEN for this book.*

Hotten's Edition of "CONTES DROLATIQUES" (Droll Tales collected from the Abbeys of Lorraine), par BALZAC. With 425 Marvellous, Extravagant, and Fantastic Woodcuts by DORÉ. Beautifully printed, thick 8vo, half morocco, Roxburghe. 12s. 6d.

*** *The most singular designs ever attempted by any artist. So crammed is the book with pictures that even the contents are adorned with thirty-three illustrations.* DIRECT application must be made to Mr. HOTTEN for this work.

GUSTAVE DORÉ'S FAVOURITE PENCIL SKETCHES.

HISTORICAL CARTOONS; or, Rough Pencillings of the World's History from the First to the Nineteenth Century. By GUSTAVE DORÉ. With admirable letterpress descriptions by THOMAS WRIGHT, F.S.A. Oblong 4to, handsome Table Book. Price 7s. 6d.

*** *This is a new book of daring and inimitable designs, which will excite considerable attention, and doubtless command a very wide circulation.*

JOHN CAMDEN HOTTEN, 74 AND 75, PICCADILLY, LONDON.

Very Important New Books.

THE COLLECTOR; Essays on Books, Newspapers,
Pictures, Inns, Authors, Doctors, Holidays, Actors, Preachers. By HENRY T. TUCKERMAN; with an Introduction by Dr. DORAN. Half morocco, 6s.

⁎⁎ *A charming volume of delightful Essays, and a Companion to John Hill Burton's "Book-Hunter."*

LITERARY COPYRIGHT. Seven Letters addressed by
permission to Earl Stanhope, D.C.L., F.R.S. By JOHN CAMDEN HOTTEN. Price 5s.

"A sensible and valuable little book."—*Athenæum.*
"We agree with Mr. Hotten."—*Saturday Review.*

OLD DRAMATISTS—NEW EDITIONS.

MARLOWE'S (Christopher) WORKS; Including his
Translations. Edited, with Notes and Introduction, by Lieut.Col. F. CUNNINGHAM. Cr. 8vo, Portrait, cloth, 4s. 6d.; cloth gilt, 5s.

MASSINGER'S (Philip) PLAYS. From the Text of WM. GIFFORD. With the addition of the Tragedy of "Believe as You List." Edited by Lieut.Col. FRANCIS CUNNINGHAM. Crown 8vo, Portrait. Cloth, 4s. 6d.; cloth gilt, 5s.

BEN JONSON'S WORKS. With Notes, Critical and Explanatory, and a Biographical Memoir by WILLIAM GIFFORD. Edited by Lieut.Col. FRANCIS CUNNINGHAM. Complete in 3 vols., crown 8vo, Portrait, cloth, 4s. 6d. each; cloth gilt, 5s. each.

LIFE AND NEWLY-DISCOVERED WRITINGS OF DANIEL
DEFOE. Comprising Several Hundred Important Essays, Pamphlets, and other Writings, now first brought to light, after many years' diligent search. By WILLIAM LEE, Esq. With Facsimiles and Illustrations. 3 vols., uniform with "Macaulay's History of England." 36s.

A VERY USEFUL BOOK.—In folio, half morocco, cloth sides, 7s. 6d.

LITERARY SCRAPS, CUTTINGS from NEWSPAPERS,
EXTRACTS, MISCELLANEA, &c. A FOLIO SCRAP-BOOK OF 340 COLUMNS, formed for the reception of Cuttings, &c., with guards.

⁎⁎ *A most useful volume, and one of the cheapest ever sold.*

THE ROSICRUCIANS; their Rites and Mysteries.
With Chapters on the Ancient Fire and Serpent Worshippers, and Explanations of the Mystic Symbols represented in the Monuments and Talismans of the Primeval Philosophers. By HARGRAVE JENNINGS. 10s. 6d.

⁎⁎ *A volume of startling facts and opinions upon this very mysterious subject, illustrated by nearly 300 engravings.*

"Curious as many of Mr. Hotten's works have been, the volume now under notice is, among them all, perhaps the most remarkable. The work purports to describe the Rites and Mysteries of the Rosicrucians. It dilates on the ancient Fire and Serpent Worshippers. The Author has certainly devoted an enormous amount of labour to these memorials of the ROSS-CROSS—otherwise the Rosicrucians."—*The Sun.*

JOHN CAMDEN HOTTEN, 74 AND 75, PICCADILLY, LONDON.

Very Important New Books.

HOGARTH'S FIVE DAYS'
Frolic; or, "Peregrinations by Land and Water." Illustrated with TINTED DRAWINGS, made by HOGARTH and SCOTT during the Journey. 4to, beautifully printed, 10s. 6d.

₊ *A graphic and most extraordinary picture of the hearty English times in which these merry artists lived.*

ACROSTICS, in Prose and
Verse. Edited by A. E. H. 12mo, gilt cloth, gilt edges, 3s.
—— SECOND SERIES, cloth gilt, 3s.
—— THIRD SERIES, cloth gilt, 3s.
—— FOURTH SERIES. With 8 Pictorial Acrostics. Cloth gilt, 3s.
—— FIFTH SERIES. An entirely New and Original Work. Cloth elegant, 4s. 6d.
—— SUPPLEMENT, under the title of "Easy Double, Historical, and Scriptural Acrostics." Cloth gilt, 3s.

₊ *Each series sold separately. These are the best volumes of Acrostics ever issued. They comprise Single, Double, Treble, and every variety of acrostic, and the set would amuse the younger members of a family for an entire winter.*

The Five Series Complete in a Case, "The Acrostic Box," price 15s.

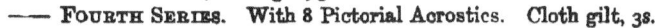

WONDERFUL CHARACTERS: Memoirs and Anecdotes
of *Remarkable and Eccentric Persons of Every Age and Nation.* From the text of HENRY WILSON and JAMES CAULFIELD. 8vo, with SIXTY-ONE FULL-PAGE ENGRAVINGS OF EXTRAORDINARY PERSONS, price 7s. 6d.

₊ *There are so many curious matters discussed in this volume, that any person who takes it up will not readily lay it down. The introduction is almost entirely devoted to a consideration of Pig-Faced Ladies, and the various stories concerning them.*

JOHN CAMDEN HOTTEN, 74 AND 75, PICCADILLY, LONDON.

Very Important New Books.

AN EPIC OF WOMEN, and other Poems. By ARTHUR W. E. O'SHAUGHNESSY. With Original Designs by Mr. J. T. NETTLESHIP. Cloth, neat, price 6s.

"What he has given us is remarkable. With its quaint title, and quaint illustrations, 'AN EPIC OF WOMEN' will be a rich treat to a wide circle of admirers."—*Athenæum*, Nov. 5, 1870.

"Combine Morris and Swinburne, and inspire the product with a fervour essentially original, and you have, as we take it, a fair notion of Mr. O'Shaughnessy's poems."—*Dispatch*, Oct. 30, 1870.

ANACREON. Illustrated by the Exquisite Designs of GIRODET. Translated by THOMAS MOORE. Bound in vellum cloth and Etruscan gold, 12s. 6d.

** *A MOST BEAUTIFUL AND CAPTIVATING VOLUME. The well-known Paris house, Firmin Didot, a few years since produced a miniature edition of these exquisite designs by the photographic process, and sold a large number at £2 per copy. The designs have been universally admired by both artists and poets.*

ECHOES FROM THE FRENCH POETS. An Anthology from BAUDELAIRE, ALFRED DE MUSSET, LAMARTINE, VICTOR HUGO, A. CHENIER, T. GAUTIER, BERANGER, NADAUD, DUPONT, PARNY, and others. By HARRY CURWEN. Fcap. 8vo, cloth, 5s.; half-morocco, 6s.

"A pleasant little volume of translations from modern French poets."—*Graphic*, Aug. 20, 1870.

FAIR ROSAMOND, and other Poems. By B. MONTGOMERIE RANKING (of the Inner Temple). Fcap. 8vo, price 6s.

JOHN CAMDEN HOTTEN, 74 AND 75, PICCADILLY, LONDON.

Very Important New Books.

CHARLES DICKENS—The Story of his Life. By the Author of "The Life of Thackeray." Price 7s. 6d., with NUMEROUS PORTRAITS AND ILLUSTRATIONS, 370 pp.

"Anecdotes seem to have poured in upon the author from all quarters... Turn where we will through these 370 pleasant pages, something worth reading is sure to meet the eye."—*The Standard*.

Dickens's Life : Another Edition, without Illustrations, uniform with the "CHARLES DICKENS EDITION," and forming a Supplementary Volume to that favourite issue, crimson cloth, 3s. 6d.

DICKENS'S SUMMER HOUSE.

Dickens's Life.—CHEAP POPULAR EDITION, in paper, 2s.

DICKENS'S SPEECHES, Literary and Social.—Now first collected. With Chapters on "Charles Dickens as a Letter Writer, Poet, and Public Reader." Price 7s. 6d., with Fine Portrait by Count D'ORSAY, 370 pages.

** "His capital speeches. Every one of them reads like a page of 'Pickwick.'"—*The Critic*.

"His speeches are as good as any of his printed writings."—*The Times*.

Dickens's Speeches.—Uniform with the "CHARLES DICKENS EDITION," and forming a Supplementary Volume to that favourite issue, crimson cloth, 3s. 6d.

Dickens's Speeches. — CHEAP EDITION, without Portrait, in paper wrapper, 2s.

HUNTED DOWN. A Story by CHARLES DICKENS. With some Account of Wainewright, the Poisoner. Price 6d.

** *A powerful and intensely thrilling story, now first printed in book-form in this country.*

JOHN CAMDEN HOTTEN, 74 AND 75, PICCADILLY, LONDON.

Very Important New Books.

For Gold and Silversmiths.
PRIVATE BOOK OF USEFUL ALLOYS AND MEMORANDA for *GOLDSMITHS* and *JEWELLERS*. By JAMES E. COLLINS, C.E., of Birmingham. Royal 16mo, 3s. 6d.
*** *The secrets of the Gold and Silversmiths' Art are here given, for the benefit of young Apprentices and Practitioners. It is an invaluable book to the Trade.*

THE STANDARD WORK ON DIAMONDS AND PRECIOUS STONES: their History, Value, and Properties; with Simple Tests for ascertaining their Reality. By HARRY EMANUEL, F.R.G.S. With numerous Illustrations, tinted and plain. New Edition. Prices brought down to the present time, full gilt, 6s.

 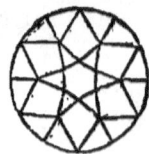 

"Will be acceptable to many readers."—*Times'* review of three columns.
"An invaluable work for buyers and sellers."—*Spectator.*
*** *This Second Edition is greatly superior to the previous one. It gives the latest market value for Diamonds and Precious Stones of every size.*

GUNTER'S MODERN CONFECTIONER. The Best Book on Confectionery and Desserts. An Entirely New Edition of this Standard Work, adapted for Private Families or Large Establishments. By WILLIAM JEANES, Chief Confectioner at Messrs. GUNTER's, Berkeley Square. With Plates, 8vo, cloth, 6s. 6d.
"All housekeepers should have it."—*Daily Telegraph.*
*** *This work has won for itself the reputation of being the Standard English Book on the preparation of all kinds of Confectionery, and on the arrangement of Desserts.*

HOUSEKEEPER'S ASSISTANT. A Collection of the most valuable Recipes, carefully written down for future use by Mrs. B——, during her Forty Years' active Service. Cloth, price 2s. 6d.
*** *As much as two guineas have been paid for a copy of this invaluable little work.*

THE YOUNG BOTANIST: *A Popular Guide to Elementary Botany.* By T. S. RALPH, of the Linnæan Society. In 1 vol., with 300 Drawings from Nature, 2s. 6d. plain; 4s. Coloured by hand.
*** *An excellent book for the young beginner. The objects selected as illustrations are either easy of access as specimens of wild plants, or are common in gardens.*

CHAMPAGNE: *its History, Manufacture, Properties,* &c. By CHARLES TOVEY, Author of "Wine and Wine Countries," "British and Foreign Spirits," &c., Cr. 8vo, numerous illustrations, 5s.
*** *A practical work, by one of the largest champagne merchants in London.*

BRIGHAM'S (Dr. A.) MENTAL EXERTION: *Its Influence on Health.* With Notes and Remarks on Dyspepsia of Literary Men. By ARTHUR LEARED, M.D. 8vo, boards, 1s. 6d.

JOHN CAMDEN HOTTEN, 74 AND 75, PICCADILLY, LONDON.

Very Important New Books.

NAPOLEON III., THE MAN OF HIS TIME:
PART I.—The STORY OF THE LIFE OF NAPOLEON III., as told by JAS. W. HASWELL.
PART II.—The SAME STORY, as told by the POPULAR CARICATURES of the past Thirty-five Years. Crown 8vo, 400 pages, 7s. 6d.

₊ *The object of this Work is to give Both Sides of the Story. The Artist has gone over the entire ground of Continental and English Caricatures for the last third of a century, and a very interesting book is the result.*

CRUIKSHANK'S COMIC ALMANACK.
A Nineteen Years' gathering of the BEST HUMOUR, the WITTIEST SAYINGS, the Drollest Quips, and the Best Things of THACKERAY, HOOD, MAYHEW, ALBERT SMITH, A'BECKETT, ROBERT BROUGH, 1835-1853. With nearly Two Thousand Woodcuts and Steel Engravings by the inimitable CRUIKSHANK, HINE, LANDELLS, &c. Two Series, Crown 8vo, each of 600 pages, price 7s. 6d. each.

₊ *A most extraordinary gathering of the best wit and humour of the past half-century. Readers can purchase one Series and judge for themselves. The work forms a "Comic History of England" for twenty years.*

JOHN CAMDEN HOTTEN, 74 AND 75, PICCADILLY, LONDON.

Very Important New Books.

Original Edition of the Famous JOE MILLER'S JESTS;
the politest Repartees, most elegant Bon-Mots, and most pleasing short Stories in the English Language. London: printed by T. Read, 1739. Remarkable facsimile. 8vo, half morocco, price 9s. 6d.

*** ONLY A VERY FEW COPIES OF THIS HUMOROUS AND RACY OLD BOOK HAVE BEEN REPRODUCED.

HISTORY OF PLAYING CARDS. With Sixty curious Illustrations, 550 pp., price 7s. 6d.

"A highly interesting volume:"—*Morning Post.*

ANECDOTES, ANCIENT AND MODERN GAMES, CONJURING, FORTUNE-TELLING AND CARD-SHARPING, SKILL AND SLEIGHT OF HAND, GAMBLING AND CALCULATION, CARTOMANCY AND CHEATING, OLD GAMES AND GAMING-HOUSES, CARD REVELS AND BLIND HOOKEY, PICQUET AND VINGT-ET-UN, WHIST AND CRIBBAGE, OLD-FASHIONED TRICKS.

SLANG DICTIONARY; or, The Vulgar Words, Street
Phrases, and "Fast" Expressions of High and Low Society; many with their Etymology, and a few with their History traced. WITH CURIOUS ILLUSTRATIONS. A New Dictionary of Colloquial English. Pp. 328, in 8vo, price 6s. 6d.

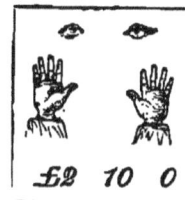

See TWO UPON TEN, *in the Dictionary*, p. 264.

"It may be doubted if there exists a more amusing volume in the English language."—*Spectator.*
"Valuable as a work of reference."—*Saturday Review.*
"All classes of society will find amusement and instruction in its pages."—*Times.*

Egyptian Hieroglyphic reʋb, to be drunk, showing the amputation of a man's leg. See under BREAKY LEG (viz. *Strong Drink*) in the Dictionary, p. 81.

CAPTAIN GROSE'S DICTIONARY of the VULGAR TONGUE,
1785. A genuine unmutilated Reprint of the First Edition. Price 8s.

*** Only a small number of copies of this very vulgar, but very curious, book have been printed for the Collectors of "Street Words" and Colloquialisms, on fine toned paper, half-bound morocco, gilt top.

JOHN CAMDEN HOTTEN, 74 AND 75, PICCADILLY, LONDON.

Very Important New Books.

THE NEW "PUNIANA" SERIES OF
CHOICE ILLUSTRATED WORKS of HUMOUR.

Elegantly printed on toned paper, full gilt, gilt edges, for the Drawing-Room, price 6s. each.

1. ***CAROLS OF COCKAYNE.*** By HENRY S. LEIGH. Vers de Société, and charming Verses descriptive of London Life. With numerous exquisite little Designs by ALFRED CONCANEN and the late JOHN LEECH. Small 4to, elegant, uniform with "Puniana," 6s.

2. ***COUNTRY-HOUSE CHARADES,*** *for Acting.* By Capt. E. C. NUGENT. With Illustrations by W. R. SNOW. Small 4to, green and gold, 6s.
*** *An entirely new book of Household Amusements. An Appendix gives the various Songs set to Music for accompaniment upon the Pianoforte.*

"AN AWFULLY JOLLY BOOK FOR PARTIES."

3. ***PUNIANA: Thoughts Wise and Otherwise.*** Best Book of Riddles and Puns ever formed. With nearly 100 exquisitely fanciful Drawings. Contains nearly 3,000 of the best Riddles and 10,000 most outrageous Puns, and is one of the most Popular Books ever issued. New Edition, uniform with the "Bab Ballads." Price 6s.

Why did Du Chaillu get so angry when he was chaffed about the Gorilla?—Why? we ask.

Why is a chrysalis like a hot roll?—You will doubtless remark, "Because it's the grub that makes the butter fly!" But see "Puniana."

Why is a wide-awake hat so called?—Because it never had a nap, and never wants one.

The *Saturday Review* says of this most amusing work:—"Enormous burlesque—unapproachable and pre-eminent. We venture to think that this very queer volume will be a favourite. It deserves to be so; and we should suggest that, to a dull person desirous to get credit with the young holiday people, it would be good policy to invest in the book, and dole it out by instalments."

NEW SOCIETY BOOK BY THE AUTHOR OF "PUNIANA."

4. ***GAMOSAGAMMON;*** or, Advice to Parties about to Connubialise. By the Hon. HUGH ROWLEY. With numerous exquisite and fanciful designs from his pencil. Small 4to, green and gold, 6s.

*** The Quaintest, Funniest, most Original Book published for a long time.

JOHN CAMDEN HOTTEN, 74 AND 75, PICCADILLY, LONDON.

Very Important New Books.

PIERCE EGAN'S "FINISH" TO "LIFE IN AND OUT OF LONDON."
Royal 8vo, cloth extra, WITH SPIRITED COLOURED ILLUSTRATIONS BY CRUIKSHANK, 21s.

⁎ An extraordinary picture of "LONDON BY NIGHT" in the Days of George the Fourth. All the strange places of Amusement around Covent Garden and in St. James's are fully described, and very queer places they were too!

LIFE IN LONDON; or, The Day and Night Scenes of
Jerry Hawthorn and Corinthian Tom. Crown 8vo. WITH THE WHOLE OF CRUIKSHANK'S VERY DROLL ILLUSTRATIONS, IN COLOURS, AFTER THE ORIGINALS. Cloth extra, 7s. 6d.

TOM AND JERRY TAKING A STROLL.

⁎ One of the most popular books ever issued. It was an immense favourite with George IV., and as a picture of London life fifty years ago was often quoted by Thackeray, who devotes one of his "Roundabout Papers" to a description of it. Clean Second-hand copies of this work always realize from £1 to £2.

VYNER'S NOTITIA VENATICA: A Treatise on Fox-
Hunting, the General Management of Hounds, and the Diseases of Dogs; Distemper and Rabies; Kennel Lameness, &c. Sixth Edition, Enlarged. By ROBERT C. VYNER, Esq., of Eathorpe Hall, Warwickshire. Royal 8vo. WITH SPIRITED ILLUSTRATIONS IN COLOURS, BY ALKEN, OF MEMORABLE FOX-HUNTING SCENES. 21s.

⁎ An Entirely New Edition of the best work extant upon Fox-Hunting.

"TOM SMITH."
REMINISCENCES OF THE LATE THOMAS ASSHETON
SMITH, Esq.; or, The Pursuits of an English Country Gentleman. By SIR JOHN E. EARDLEY WILMOT, Bart. With Illustrations COLOURED and PLAIN. New Edition, uniform with Nimrod's "Chase, Turf, and Road." Price 7s. 6d.

FINE OLD HUNTING BOOKS, with Coloured Plates.
MR. JORROCKS'S JAUNTS AND JOLLITIES.
LIFE AND ADVENTURES OF JACK MYTTON.
ANALYSIS OF THE HUNTING FIELD.
LIFE OF A SPORTSMAN. By NIMROD.

Apply to Mr. Hotten DIRECT for these books.

JOHN CAMDEN HOTTEN, 74 AND 75, PICCADILLY, LONDON.

Very Important New Books.

HISTORY OF CARICATURE AND THE GROTESQUE in
Art, Literature, Sculpture, and Painting, from the Earliest Times to the Present Day. By THOMAS WRIGHT, F.S.A. (Author of "A Caricature History of the Georges.") 4to, profusely illustrated by FAIRHOLT. 21s.

∗ *A valuable historical, and at the same time most entertaining work. The author's first idea was to call it a "History of Comic Literature and Art in Great Britain." The illustrations are full of interest.*

GEORGE III. WONDERING HOW THE APPLES GOT INSIDE THE DUMPLINGS.

CARICATURE HISTORY OF THE GEORGES (House of
Hanover). Very Entertaining Book of 640 pages, with 400 Pictures, Caricatures, Squibs, Broadsides, Window Pictures. By T. WRIGHT, F.S.A. 7s. 6d.

∗ *Companion Volume to "History of Signboards." Reviewed in almost every English journal with the highest approbation.*

"A set of caricatures such as we have in Mr. Wright's volume brings the surface of the age before us with a vividness that no prose writer, even of the highest power, could emulate. Macaulay's most brilliant sentence is weak by the side of the little woodcut from Gillray, which gives us Burke and Fox."—*Saturday Review.*

"A more amusing work of its kind was never issued."—*Art Journal.*

"It is emphatically one of the liveliest of books, as also one of the most interesting. It has the twofold merit of being at once amusing and edifying. The 600 odd pages which make up the goodly volume are doubly enhanced by some 400 illustrations, of which a dozen are full-page ones."—*Morning Post.*

LARGE PAPER EDITION, 4to, only 100 printed, on extra fine paper, wide margins, for the lovers of choice books, with extra Portraits, half morocco (a capital book to illustrate), 30s.

A Companion Table Book to "Leech's Sketches."

MAIDEN HOURS AND MAIDEN WILES. Designed by
"BEAUJOLAIS" (CAPTAIN HANS BUSK). A SERIES OF REMARKABLY CLEVER SKETCHES, showing the Occupations of a Fashionable Young Lady at All Hours of the Day. With appropriate Text. Folio, half morocco, blue and gold, gilt edges, 10s. 6d.

JOHN CAMDEN HOTTEN, 74 AND 75, PICCADILLY, LONDON.

Very Important New Books.

A CLEVER AND BRILLIANT BOOK,
Companion to the "Bon Gaultier Ballads."
PUCK ON PEGASUS. By
H. CHOLMONDELEY PENNELL. In 4to, printed within an India-paper tone, and elegantly bound, gilt, gilt edges, price 10s. 6d. only.

₊ *This most amusing work has already passed through Five Editions, receiving everywhere the highest praise as "a clever and brilliant book." To no other work of the present day have so many distinguished Artists contributed Illustrations. To the designs of* GEORGE CRUIKSHANK, JOHN LEECH, JULIAN PORTCH, "PHIZ," *and other Artists,* SIR NOEL PATON, MILLAIS, JOHN TENNIEL, RICHARD DOYLE, *and* M. ELLEN EDWARDS, *have now contributed several exquisite pictures, thus making the New Edition—which is Twice the Size of the old one, and contains irresistibly funny pieces — the best book for the Drawing-room table now published.*

AUSTIN'S (Alfred) THE SEASON: A Satire.
Elegantly bound for the Drawing-room, 5s

₊ *An entirely New Edition of this famous Work, it having been out of print seven years.*

SIGNBOARDS: Their History. With Anecdotes of Famous
Taverns and Remarkable Characters. By JACOB LARWOOD and JOHN CAMDEN HOTTEN. "A book which will delight all."—*Spectator*. Fourth Edition, 580 pp., price 7s. 6d. only.

From the "Times."

"It is not fair on the part of a reviewer to pick out the plums of an author's book, thus filching away his cream, and leaving little but skim-milk remaining; but, even if we were ever so maliciously inclined,

BULL AND MOUTH.

From the "Times."

we could not in the present instance pick out all Messrs. Larwood and Hotten's plums, because the good things are so numerous as to defy the most wholesale depredation."—*Review of three columns.*

₊ *Nearly 100 most curious illustrations on wood are given, showing the various old signs which were formerly hung from taverns and other houses.*

ROMANCE OF THE ROD: An Anecdotal History of the
Birch, in Ancient and Modern Times. With some quaint Illustrations. Crown 8vo, handsomely printed. [*In preparation*

JOHN CAMDEN HOTTEN, 74 AND 75, PICCADILLY, LONDON.

Very Important New Books.

THE FAMOUS "DOCTOR SYNTAX'S" THREE TOURS.
One of the most amusing and Laughable Books ever published. WITH THE WHOLE OF ROWLANDSON'S VERY DROLL FULL-PAGE ILLUSTRATIONS, IN COLOURS, AFTER THE ORIGINAL DRAWINGS. Comprising the well-known TOURS—

1. In Search of the Picturesque. | 2. In Search of Consolation.
3. In Search of a Wife.

The Three Series Complete and Unabridged in One Handsome Volume with a Life of this industrious Author—the English Le Sage—now first written by JOHN CAMDEN HOTTEN. This Edition contains the whole of the original, hitherto sold for 31s. 6d., now published at 7s. 6d. only.

UNIFORM WITH "WONDERFUL CHARACTERS."

REMARKABLE TRIALS AND NOTORIOUS CHARACTERS.
From "Half-Hanged Smith," 1700, to Oxford who shot at the Queen, 1840. By CAPTAIN L. BENSON. With spirited full-page Engravings by PHIZ. 8vo, 550 pages, 7s. 6d.

*** *A Complete Library of Sensation Literature! There are plots enough here to produce a hundred "exciting" Novels, and at least five hundred "powerful" Magazine Stories. The book will be appreciated by all readers whose taste lies in this direction. Phiz's pictures are fully equal to those in "Master Humphrey's Clock."*

A Keepsake for Smokers.
"THE SMOKER'S TEXT-BOOK." By J. HAMER, F.R.S.L.
Exquisitely printed from "silver-faced" type, cloth, very neat, gilt edges, 2s. 6d., post free.

"A pipe is a great comforter, a pleasant soother. The man who smokes, thinks like a sage, and acts like a Samaritan."
—*Bulwer.*

"A tiny volume, dedicated to the votaries of the weed; beautifully printed on toned paper, in, we believe, the smallest type ever made (cast especially for show at the Great Exhibition in Hyde Park), but very clear, notwithstanding its minuteness.... The pages sing, in various styles, the praises of tobacco. Amongst the writers laid under contribution are Bulwer, Kingsley, Charles Lamb, Thackeray, Isaac Browne, Cowper, and Byron."
—*The Field.*

18

THE TRUE CONSOLER.

HE who doth not smoke hath either known no great griefs, or refuseth himself the softest consolation, next to that which comes from heaven "What softer than woman?" whispers the young reader. Young reader, woman teases as well as consoles. Woman makes half the sorrows which sh· boasts the privilege to soothe. Woman consoles us, it is true, while we are young and handsome; when we are old and ugly, woman snubs and scolds us. On the whole, than, woman in this scale the weed in that. Jupiter, hang out thy balance, and weigh them both; and if thou give the preference to woman all I can say is, the next time Juno ruffles thee—O Jupiter! try the weed.
BULWER'S "What will he do with it?"

JOHN CAMDEN HOTTEN, 74 AND 75, PICCADILLY, LONDON.

Very Important New Books.

ORIGINAL EDITION OF BLAKE'S WORKS.

NOTICE.—Mr. HOTTEN has prepared a few Facsimile Copies *(exact as to paper and printing—the water-colour drawings being filled in by an artist)* of the ORIGINAL EDITION OF BLAKE'S " MARRIAGE OF HEAVEN AND HELL." 4to, price 30s., half morocco.

"Blake is a real name, I assure you, and a most extraordinary man he is, if he still be living. He is the Blake whose wild designs accompany a splendid edition of 'Blair's Grave.' He paints in water-colours marvellous strange pictures—visions of his brain—which he asserts he has seen. They have great merit. I must look upon him as one of the most extraordinary persons of the age."—CHARLES LAMB.

EMERSON. The Uncollected Writings, Essays, and
Lectures of RALPH WALDO EMERSON. With Introductory Preface by MONCURE CONWAY. 2 vols.,8vo. By Arrangement with Mr. EMERSON.

INFELICIA. Poems by Adah Isaacs Menken. With
NUMEROUS GRACEFUL DESIGNS ON WOOD. Dedicated, by permission, to CHARLES DICKENS, with Photographic Facsimile of his Letter, and a Portrait of the Authoress. In green and gold, 5s. 6d.

"A pathetic little volume exquisitely got up."—*Sun*.

"Few, if any, could have guessed the power and beauty of the thoughts that possessed her soul, and found expression in language at once pure and melodious."—*Press.*

"There is a passionate richness about many of the poems which is almost startling."—*Sunday Times.*

"What can we say of this gifted and wayward woman, the existence of whose better nature will be suggested for the first time to many by the posthumous disclosure of this book? We do not envy the man who, reading it, has only a sneer for its writer; nor the woman who finds it in her heart to turn away with averted face."—*New York Round Table.*

"An amusing little book, unhappily posthumous, which a distinguished woman has left as a legacy to mankind and the age."—*Saturday Review.*

Fcap. 8vo, 450 pages, with fine Portrait and Autograph, 7s. 6d.

WALT WHITMAN'S POEMS. (Leaves of Grass, Drum-
Taps, &c.) Selected and Edited by WILLIAM MICHAEL ROSSETTI.

"Whitman is a poet who bears and needs to be read as a whole, and then the volume and torrent of his power carry the disfigurements along with it and away. He is really a fine fellow."—*Chambers's Journal*, in a very long notice.

THE EARTHWARD PILGRIMAGE. By MONCURE CONWAY.
Cr. 8vo, 400 pages, cloth, neat, 7s. 6d.

*** *This volume has excited considerable discussion, as it advances many entirely new views upon the life hereafter. The titles to some of the chapters will convey an idea of the contents of the work:*—"*How I left the world to come for that which is.*"

JOHN CAMDEN HOTTEN, 74 AND 75, PICCADILLY, LONDON.

Very Important New Books.

MR. SWINBURNE'S ESSAY.

⁎ *"A wonderful literary performance."*—*"Splendour of style and majestic beauty of diction never surpassed."*

WILLIAM BLAKE: A Critical Essay. With facsimile Paintings, Coloured by Hand, from the Original Drawings painted by Blake and his Wife. Thick 8vo, pp. 350, 16s.

"An extraordinary work: violent, extravagant, perverse, calculated to startle, to shock, and to alarm many readers, but abounding in beauty, and characterized by intellectual grasp. . . . His power of word-painting is often truly wonderful — sometimes, it must be admitted, in excess, but always full of matter, form, and colour, and instinct with a sense of vitality."—*Daily News*, Feb. 12, 1868.

"It is in every way worthy of Mr. Swinburne's high fame. In no prose work can be found passages of keener poetry, or more finished grace, or more impressive harmony. Strong, vigorous, and musical, the style sweeps on like a river."—*The Sunday Times*, Jan. 12, 1868.

MR. SWINBURNE'S SONG OF ITALY. Fcap. 8vo, toned paper, cloth, price 3s. 6d.

⁎ The *Athenæum* remarks of this poem—"Seldom has such a chant been heard, so full of glow, strength, and colour."

MR. SWINBURNE'S POEMS AND BALLADS. FOURTH EDITION. Price 9s.

MR. SWINBURNE'S NOTES ON HIS POEMS, and on the Reviews which have appeared upon them. Price 1s.

MR. SWINBURNE'S ATALANTA IN CALYDON. New Edition. Fcap. 8vo, price 6s.

MR. SWINBURNE'S CHASTELARD. A Tragedy. New Edition. Price 7s.

MR. SWINBURNE'S QUEEN MOTHER AND ROSAMOND. New Edition. Fcap. 8vo, price 5s.

MR. SWINBURNE'S BOTHWELL. A New Poem.
[*In preparation.*

JOHN CAMDEN HOTTEN, 74 AND 75, PICCADILLY, LONDON.

Very Important New Books.

⁎ Mr. HOTTEN *is enabled to afford most material and important assistance to all interested in Genealogical Inquiries, difficult Pedigree Researches, or in the compilation of Family Histories. He has the following*

FAMILY HISTORIES FOR SALE:—

FORSTER and FOSTER FAMILIES. 4to. Illustrations, 31s. 6d.
BAIRD FAMILY. Royal 8vo. Facsimiles. 10s. 6d.
CHICHESTER and RALEIGH FAMILIES. 4to. Illustrations, 21s.; with Arms emblazoned, 31s. 6d.
MILLAIS FAMILY. With Etchings by Millais. 28s.
WASHINGTON FAMILY. Preparing.
COLE FAMILY.
STUART FAMILY. 8vo, half morocco. 8s. 6d.
CHICHELE FAMILY. (Contains Pedigrees of many other Families.) 4to. 17s. 6d.

ROLL OF CAERLAVEROCK, with the Arms of the Knights and others present at the Siege of the Castle in Scotland, A.D. 1300. Emblazoned in Gold and Colours, 4to, 12s.

MAGNA CHARTA. EXACT FACSIMILE of the Original Document in the British Museum. With ARMS AND SEALS OF THE BARONS EMBLAZONED IN GOLD AND COLOURS. A.D. 1215. 5s.

⁎ *Copied by express permission, and the only correct drawing of the Great Charter ever taken. A full translation, with notes, price 6d. The Charter framed and glazed in carved oak, 22s. 6d.*

ROLL OF BATTLE ABBEY: A List of the Normans who came over with William the Conqueror, and settled in this Country, A.D. 1066-67. WITH ARMS OF THE BARONS EMBLAZONED IN GOLD AND COLOURS. Price 5s.

⁎ *A most curious document, and of the greatest interest to all of Norman descent. Framed and glazed in carved oak, 22s. 6d.*

WARRANT TO EXECUTE CHARLES I. Exact Facsimile, with the 59 Signatures of Regicides, and Seals. Price 2s.; by post, 2s. 4d.

⁎ *Very curious, and copied by express permission. In carved oak and glazed, 14s. 6d.*

WARRANT TO EXECUTE MARY QUEEN OF SCOTS. Exact Facsimile, with Signature of Queen Elizabeth, and Great Seal of England. Price 2s.; by post, 2s. 4d.

⁎ *Very curious, and copied by express permission. In carved oak and glazed, 14s. 6d.*

JOHN CAMDEN HOTTEN, 74 AND 75, PICCADILLY, LONDON

Very Important New Books.

HANDBOOK OF FAMILY HISTORY OF THE ENGLISH
COUNTIES: Descriptive Account of 20,000 most Curious and Rare Books, Old Tracts, Ancient Manuscripts, Engravings, and Privately-printed Family Papers, relating to the History of almost every Landed Estate and Old English Family in the Country; interspersed with nearly Two Thousand Original Anecdotes, Topographical and Antiquarian Notes. By JOHN CAMDEN HOTTEN. Nearly 350 pages, very neat, price 5s.

** *By far the largest collection of English and Welsh Topography and Family History ever formed. Each article has a small price affixed, for the convenience of those who may desire to possess any book or tract that interests them.*

CAXTON'S STATUTES OF HENRY VII., 1489.
Edited by JOHN RAE, Esq., Fellow of the Royal Institution. The Earliest known Volume of Printed Statutes, and remarkable as being in English. MARVELLOUS FACSIMILE, from the rare original. Small folio, half morocco, £1 11s. 6d.

THE BEST HANDBOOK of HERALDRY.
Profusely Illustrated with Plates and Woodcuts. By JOHN E. CUSSANS. In crown 8vo, pp. 360, in emblazoned gold cover, with copious Index, 7s. 6d.

** *This volume, beautifully printed on toned paper, contains not only the ordinary matter to be found in the best books on the science of Armory, but several other subjects hitherto unnoticed. Amongst these may be mentioned:—1. Directions for Tracing Pedigrees. 2. Deciphering Ancient MSS., Illustrated by Alphabets and Facsimiles. 3. The Appointment of Liveries. 4. Continental and American Heraldry, &c.*

Best Guide to Reading Old MSS., Records, &c.
WRIGHT'S COURT HAND RESTORED;
or, Student's Assistant in Reading Old Deeds, Charters, Records, &c. Half morocco, 10s. 6d.

** *A New Edition, corrected, of an invaluable work to all who have occasion to consult Old MSS., Deeds, Charters, &c. It contains a series of Facsimiles of Old MSS. from the Time of the Conqueror, Tables of Contractions and Abbreviations, Ancient Surnames, &c.*

LISTS OF THE ROMAN CATHOLICS AND RECUSANTS IN
YORKSHIRE, temp. James I. (A.D. 1604). Edited, with Copious Genealogical Notes, by EDWARD PEACOCK, F.S.A. (Editor of "Army Lists of the Roundheads and Cavaliers, 1642"). 4to, elegantly printed, 12s. 6d.

JOHN CAMDEN HOTTEN, 74 AND 75, PICCADILLY, LONDON.

Very Important New Books.

Hotten's "Golden Library"
OF THE BEST AUTHORS.

₊ *A charming collection of Standard and Favourite Works, elegantly printed in Handy Volumes, uniform with the Tauchnitz Series, and published at exceedingly low prices. The New Volumes are—*

ROCHEFOUCAULD.—*Reflections and Moral Maxims.* 1s.; cloth, 1s. 6d. Essay by SAINTE-BEUVE.

SHELLEY.————*Poetical Works.* From the Author's Original Editions. First Series, QUEEN MAB and EARLY POEMS. 1s. 8d.; in cloth, 2s. 2d.

HOLMES. ————*Autocrat of the Breakfast Table.* 1s.; cloth, 1s. 6d.

THE CLERGY ————*The Book of Clerical Anecdotes and* Pulpit Eccentricities. 1s. 4d.; cloth, 1s. 10d.

CHARLES LAMB.——*The Essays of Elia.* Complete. Both Series. 1s.; cloth, 1s. 6d.

DICKENS.————*Life.* By the Author of the "Life of Thackeray." 2s.

DICKENS.————*Speeches upon Literary and Social* Topics. 2s.
"His Speeches are as good as any of his printed writings."—*The Times.*

ARTEMUS WARD.—*In London;* with the "PUNCH" Letters. 1s. 6d.; cloth, 2s. 6d.

TENNYCON. ————*Old Prose Stories of Idylls of the* King. 1s.; cloth, 1s. 6d.

DISRAELI'S, GLADSTONE'S, AND BRIGHT'S SPEECHES in separate vols., at 1s. 4d.; cloth, 1s. 10d.
Comprise all the Important Speeches of these Statesmen during the past 25 years.

CARLYLE.————*On the Choice of Books.* 1s.; cl. 1s. 6d.
Should be read and re-read by every young man in the three kingdoms.

HOLMES. ————*Professor at the Breakfast Table.* 1s.; cloth, 1s. 6d.

LEIGH HUNT. ————*Tale for a Chimney Corner, and* other Essays. 1s. 4d.; cloth, 1s. 10d.

HOOD. ————*Whims and Oddities.* 80 Illustrations. 2 Series, Complete. 1s.; cloth, 1s. 6d.

LELAND. ————*Hans Breitmann's Ballads,* Complete. 1s.; cloth, 1s. 6d.

www.ingramcontent.com/pod-product-compliance
Lightning Source LLC
Chambersburg PA
CBHW021345230426

43666CB00006B/410